TALES OF OLD
AUSTRALIA

TALES OF OLD AUSTRALIA

BILL BEATTY

LIFETIME DISTRIBUTORS
"The Book People"

Published for
Lifetime Distributors
6/8 Victoria Avenue, Castle Hill, New South Wales 2154
by
Murray Child & Company Pty Ltd
64 Suffolk Avenue, Collaroy, New South Wales, 2097
Edited by Carolyn Child
Cover design by Emma Seymour
Text design by Murray Child
© The Estate of the late Bill Beatty
Printed by Australian Print Group, Maryborough, Victoria

National Library of Australia Catalogue Card No. and ISBN
1 86436 013 5

Cover illustration: Frank Mahoney, Australia, 1862–1917,
Rounding up a straggler, 1889, oil on canvas, 91.5 x 127.6 cm,
Art Gallery of New South Wales, Purchased 1889

The line illustrations used throughout this book
were reproduced from engravings in
Cassell's Picturesque Australasia, edited by E. E. Morris, 1889 and
Australasia Illustrated, edited by Andrew Garran, 1892.

CONTENTS

PREFACE TO THE FIRST EDITION

Australia's past has a pungent flavour all its own. It may remind us at times of a little of America's covered-wagon saga, at other times of the pioneer era in New Zealand, but essentially the ingredients differ from all others. The rate of change in the Australian way of life has been so much accelerated in the last few decades that many of the stories and traditions which were once part of its fibre have been forgotten. This is a pity. The Australian character is unique; some of its qualities have their roots in our history, outlandish though they may sometimes appear to those of other countries.

It is arguable whether a nation's formal history is any more important than its indigenous stories of the past. In practice, the two are probably inter-dependent and complementary, each acquiring colour and weight from the other. Anybody wishing to understand what makes Australia the kind of country it is, and Australians the kind of people they are, undoubtedly needs to know the essential facts about the first settlement in this country a community which has had no counterpart. An astonishing conglomeration of patriots and pickpockets, forgers and free settlers, the highly learned and the illiterate, rum profiteers, the fettered and the free. One also has equal need to know the stories not always told in the history books. For the full and rounded picture of Australia one must be familiar with its formal history, its folk tales, stories and traditions, and the Australian character.

As early as Governor Macquarie's day the native-born white Australian—'currency lads' or 'wild colonials', to use two of their titles of that time—were spoken of as 'a new type, tall, loose limbed, fair, and, though strong, less athletic-looking than Englishmen of the upper classes. None denied their versatility with horses or on shipboard.' The Australian of later generations was frequently referred to as wild and undisciplined. That reputation fol-lowed him during the Boer War and World War I; yet it has been said that even larrikinism is an ebullition of animal spirit which, properly applied and trained, may produce heroes.

The call of gold, from the 1850s onward for several decades, brought men of physical strength and hardy independence from all over the world. Many

vi

types and classes of people, predominantly English, Irish and Scottish, have gone to make up the Australian people. The country has moulded them to a certain uniformity; distinguished traits of country, county and class have been all but lost in a local accent, quite unconsciously acquired.

'Old soldiers never die!' and neither will the swagmen, the bullockies, the boundary-riders, and the rest of the vanished and vanishing characters who once seemed as inseparable from the Australian outback as the emu and the kangaroo. These odd, sometimes uncouth figures are among the immortals. Their reign may have been brief, but they are enshrined as imperishably in the annals of their country as the gods and heroes of ancient Greece. However much sophisticated suburbia may wish it otherwise, the favourite picture of Australia in the imagination of the outside world is that of 'wide open spaces' with bushmen boiling billies of tea and sundowners humping their blueys across endless miles of saltbush plains.

When Governor Phillip came to this country he found it a hard, forbidding land from which he could win no sustenance. Convicts and soldiers alike were afraid of it. But fear was overcome, and in growing numbers men of strength and energy and vision fought against the unknown and made war on drought and flood. And while they worked and thrived, new generations of Australians came into being.

Tales of Old Australia is neither a detailed recital of historic events nor a full account of stories of an Australia that has passed. It is a random selection of material ranging from Captain Cook to World War II. Some of it history retold, some of it in the recollections of old-timers, some of it facts gathered first-hand, but all served plainly for what it is—the good honest fare of story-telling.

What emerges, I hope, is a many sided picture of the old Australia—warts and all. The once familiar figures of the old blade-shearers, camel-drivers, the fossickers, the shanty-keepers, the river skippers, the drover in his saddle from dawn till dusk for months on end, patiently convoying huge mobs of cattle along the stock-routes 'on the hoof' a thousand miles or more ... now vanishing from the scene as road trains take over, carrying the beasts as far in a day as they could walk in three weeks.

Not all the stories are pleasant ones; often they tell of incredible hardships, mining disasters, or heart-rending sea disasters. Because of the very nature of these tales, it would be ill-becoming to attempt to clothe them with an elegance of literary style; rather is their presentation in the form of what may be described as a home-spun simplicity.

BILL BEATTY, 1966

PUBLISHER'S NOTE

Bill Beatty was a popular journalist, author, naturalist and broad-caster during the 1950s and 1960s who died in 1970? His knowledge of Australiana was boundless and he had a fascinating and entertaining way of portraying it in print.

From the rich collection of material gathered from his many journeys around the Australian continent, he wrote twelve absorbing and informative books, many of which were translated and published in Europe. *Tales of Old Australia* was first published in 1966 and was reprinted numbers of times but by the mid-1970s it had sadly disappeared from the shelves and until recently was almost forgotten. Ernestine Hill wrote of him 'I have followed with admiration the work of Bill Beatty for many years. His perception of matters of universal interest, the lively imagination and dramatic quality he lends to the leaf of a tree or an aboriginal legend, a convict mutiny or a coral reef, have won for him a unique place among our writers of Australia with a zest of brevity and humour that appeals to everyone...'

The stories in this book are as fresh and interesting today as the day they were written. Bill Beatty captured the very essence of the early days of Australia and the passage of time since he wrote these stories, far from dulling their focus has probably sharpened it; the reader is intimately involved with everyday events of the last two centuries, witnessing gold robberies, shipwrecks, mining disasters and all manner of dramatic and tragic occurrences which would be fascinating enough if fiction but positively riveting when seen as fact.

I am pleased to be able to bring the work of this fine writer to a new generation of readers and am confident that it will find a permanent place in the folk literature of our country.

MURRAY CHILD

Old days, Old ways

Yuletides of Yore; The Rum Hospital; Matrimonial Matters;
Baked Heads from New Zealand; Curious Clubs; South of Sydney Town;
The Roaring Nineties; Cobb and Co; Woes of the early Governors;
The Iron Horse; Tramway Topics

YULETIDES OF YORE

Some of the Christmas celebrations of Australia's early years are worth recalling. Gone are the days of plum puddings boiled in communal coppers, of home-brewed brandy and overproof rum, of duels and quadrilles, and presents of gold.

Australia's history might have been very different if a gale had sprung up on Christmas Day, 1768. On that day the *Endeavour* was sailing down toward Tierra del Fuego and young Mr Banks entered in his diary: 'Christmas Day all good Christians, that is to say all good hands, got abominably drunk so that all through the night there was scarce a sober man in the ship. Weather, thank God, very moderate, or the Lord knows what would have become of us.'

When the Christmas of 1769 came, the *Endeavour* was near the Three Kings, off the New Zealand coast. On Christmas Eve Joseph Banks had gone out in his boat and shot several gannets, or 'solan geese' as he calls them. These were made into goose-pie for the Christmas dinner and eaten 'with great approbation'. And in the evening 'all hands were as drunk as our forefathers used to be upon like occasions'.

Goose-pie, recorded by Banks, featured also on the festive menu of another explorer, James Kelly, the first man to sail round the island State of Tasmania. On Christmas Day, 1815, he and his crew of four in their whaleboat found themselves weather-bound in a little inlet on the west coast of Tasmania, north of Port Davey. His diary says, 'This day we had a glorious dinner. Two black swans, one roasted (stuck up), the other a sea-pie—a three-decker—in the large iron pot. It was first-rate.' Christmas of 1788 found the First Fleet lumbering eastward across the Southern Ocean toward Van Dieman's Land. David Collins, the historian of the earliest days, says, 'We complied, as far as was in our power, with the good old English custom and partook of a better dinner this day than usual; but the weather was too rough to permit of much social enjoyment.'

The second Australian Christmas found the motley band of pioneers in happier circumstances. The bush around Sydney Cove had been cleared, houses had been erected for the military officers and wattle and daub huts for convicts. On this occasion we are told that 'Christmas Day was observed with proper ceremony. Mr Johnson preached a sermon adapted to the occasion, and the major part of the officers were afterwards entertained at dinner by the Governor.'

There was at least one lady in the infant settlement, however, who, theoretically, did not enjoy this particular season. She had been found guilty, a few days before Christmas, of receiving stolen property from a convict thief, and, the convicts being assembled, this woman had her hair shaved off and was then clothed with a canvas frock on which was painted in large letters RSG, which signified 'receiver of stolen goods'.

She was threatened with more severe punishment if seen without her unique frock.

In December, 1791, supplies were so low that the rations had to be cut. The best Governor Phillip could do was to allow a pound of flour to each woman in the settlement. But, if the men had to tighten their belts that Christmas Day, they made certain cheer of another sort. The stores at Parramatta were broken into, and some twenty-two gallons of liquor spirited away.

The Christmas of 1803 saw an odd little community of marines, convicts, and free settlers—Victoria's first white settlement—sitting down to Christmas dinner in the bushland of Sullivan's Bay. The location has been identified as lying between the two points now known as The Sisters, half a mile cast of Sorrento. The strangely assorted company celebrating Victoria's first Christmas was presided over by Lieutenant-Governor David Collins, impatient to move his settlement to Van Diemen's Land. Prominent, also, was the devastating Mrs Powers, a convict's wife who enjoyed all the privileges, if not the legal title, of His Excellency's lady. Though Mrs Powers scarcely left the Governor's side, she bestowed many a coquettish smile on his officers.

Prominent, too, was the roistering, hunting and wine-bibbing Reverend Robert (Bobby) Knopwood, chaplain to the expedition. Now that he was well in his cups the fun-loving parson, as was his wont on such occasions, was recounting how he had dissipated a £90,000 fortune at the Prince Regent's gaming tables. Parson 'Bobby' was an extraordinary character. In Van Diemen's Land he adopted an orphan girl named Mary Mack, and she kept his house alive with her childish prattle. As she grew up, the parson kept off any suitors with a shotgun. In spite of him she married very young, but died soon after the birth of her second child.

At least two of those present at this memorable Christmas dinner did not enter wholeheartedly into the caperings of His Excellency and his staff. The strict and upright Captain Daniel Woodriff regarded the goings-on as rather unseemly, and Lieutenant Tuckey, who to the disgust of the Governor had praised the richness and fertility of the Port Phillip country as being suitable for settlement, felt himself 'on the outer'.

11

The merrymaking did not disturb the slumber of William James Hobart Thorn, infant son of a marine sergeant who had been christened that morning, with His Excellency and Mrs Powers as godparents. Young William was yet to know that he was the first child to he christened in the colony. A few yards away among the convicts and their families making their own fun was a wild eleven-year-old youngster named Johnny Fawkner, fated to succeed in later years in founding a colony where this present company of marines, soldiers, and convicts had failed.

One thing must be said in His Excellency's favour. He saw to it that everyone, convicts not excepted, had equal share of a rattling good Christmas dinner: pork, roast duck, pigeon pie, kangaroo-tail soup, with liberal helpings of fresh vegetables—green peas, beans, potatoes, and sweet corn. The rich plum pudding was boiled in a big communal copper erected specially for the purpose. Liquid refreshments included a copious supply of overproof rum.

A few weeks later the Governor and his company packed up and left for Van Diemen's Land. When years later free and lusty pioneers came to colonise Victoria, they, too, kept up the Christmas tradition. Festive cheer was passed over the counter of Fawkner's Tavern as far back as 1837, but Melbourne's first Christmas festival was held two years later at St Patrick's Hall, on Christmas Eve. Organised by the German Union, British colonists stood side by side with German settlers as they sang this specially composed verse:

But now we've quitted our dear Fatherland,
O let us form a strong fraternal band;
And our new brethren will hand extend,
For the brave Briton is the German's friend;
This land call yours—
For fair Australia is the German's home.

But while they sang of fraternity for ever on that Christmas Eve, the Yarra was at flood height. Soon water was swirling along Elizabeth Street in great volume. Squatters in town for a Christmas spree rowed about Elizabeth and Swanston streets in boats; some of the merrymakers were drowned.

Christmas celebrations of that same year, 1839, were responsible for Melbourne's first duel. Mr Peter Snodgrass and Mr William Ryrie were the principals, and they chose the present site of Spencer Street railway station to settle their 'cup of difference'. Because the nearest duelling pistols were at Heidelberg, one of the seconds was forced into a midnight dash on horseback. When he eventually galloped back with the firearms, it was found that there was no ammunition. It had been exploded when Melbourne's one ammunition shop was blown up on Christmas Eve.

Nothing daunted, the second immediately turned his horse's head toward the home of a militia officer. The officer's wife, awakened by the noise, came downstairs and demanded that the intruder should return the gunpowder he had pocketed. In the argument that followed she tried to pull the pocket from his coat. Determined not to yield, the second left hastily with the lady of the house retaining most of the coat, but not the precious pocket. And so the second returned to the scene, torn but triumphant. All was now ready but, unfortunately, one duellist, from over-excitement, shot himself in the big toe just before the signal was given to fire. The disappointed audience thereupon spent the rest of the ammunition with the attendant doctor's bell-topper (hat) as a target.

The year 1851 saw Victoria's 'gold Christmas'. New discoveries had caused a sensation in the colony and elsewhere, even overseas. Men gave friends nuggets of gold instead of Christmas cards in token of goodwill. One digger gave his horse a Christmas present of gold shoes. Another had a Christmas dinner of five pound-note sandwiches. It was a good Christmas, too, for policemen and postmen. With everyone rushing to the goldfields, the Government was at its wit's end to keep employees at their posts. The obvious course was taken: wages were raised by fifty per cent.

To find a distinctive Australian Christmas in earlier years one would have to leave the towns and go into the country. There, conditions permitted only an occasional celebration, to be the more enjoyed on that account, and Christmas was the big occasion. Weeks beforehand the head of the house smoke cured a couple of hams and stored them in the big kitchen chimney. Such bush-cured hams would last for years, not like the hams you buy today which, unless under refrigeration, will not keep for more than a couple of weeks.

On Christmas Eve a kangaroo was killed, so there was kangaroo-tail soup on the menu. Mother and her eldest daughter would be busy for days ahead, particularly in the kitchen. The main dish consisted of turkey, reared on the farm, and there were fowls baked also for those who preferred them. Instead of the latter, some bush families served wonga pigeons, satin-birds, parrots and quail, all of which were delicious eating. Some, also, served baked bandicoot, which was just like sucking-pig. Wombat ham was another favourite.

Wildlife was not only plentiful, but legally unprotected. Black swans, flying-foxes, possums, and goannas, all went into the pot. So did the koala, on occasion. In the 1890s Gundaroo Bullock was the name given to baked koala, and Grabben Gullen pie was a hollowed-out pumpkin filled with possum meat and roasted.

The Christmas pudding was taken to the table in the traditional style of old England, with flaming sauce all round it. The sauce was made from home-brewed brandy, using cherries grown on the farm. 'Plumb cake', which was given pride of place on every Christmas table, great or small, was of course the forerunner of the modern Christmas cake, rich with butter and 'plumbs' (i.e., raisins) and laced with spirits. The icing on the cake was made from manna, which was gathered under the manna gums. Manna mixed with milk made a splendid icing.

Guests arrived in bullock or horse drays, or on horseback. The spring dray was a modern luxury few could afford. At large celebrations the gargantuan repast would be followed by a dance. The floor was cleared: the 'floor' being earth beaten nearly to the consistency of concrete by countless feet, making it an excellent dancing surface. To the strains of a concertina or fiddle, everyone joined in the quadrilles, polkas, and the varsovienne. Barrels of grog on tap supplied the heavy demand for liquid refreshment, and it was not until the sun had peeped over the horizon that guests thought of home.

In more modern times there may be people who remember a pleasant Christmas custom which time and progress have all but obliterated. On Christmas Eve, or before, one would see carts laden with sapling trees passing along city streets. The trees were sold to shopkeepers, who attached one to each of their verandah posts, giving the streets a festive air. The saplings' usefulness did not end here, for they were collected and used for making bonfires on New Year's Eve. Once at Cooktown, North Queensland, the writer saw bush-foliage trees tied to verandah posts of the shops and lending an air of festivity to the celebrations.

One wonders if there is still a household where, as the guest enters on Christmas Day, he is expected to greet his host and hostess with the old lay:

> *God bless the master of this house,*
> *And bless the mistress true;*
> *And all the little children around the table, too.*
> *Your pockets full of money and your cellars full of beer,*
> *And we wish you a Merry Christmas and a Happy New Year.*

THE RUM HOSPITAL

Australia's first general hospital was shipped from England in sections and assembled in Sydney. Twenty years later the structure was in such poor shape that Governor Macquarie realised that he would have to do something about a new building. His great difficulty was lack of finance, but while he was struggling with the problem it was solved for him in quite an ingenious manner. Two men, Graham Blaxcell and Alexander Riley, approached His Excellency and offered to build the hospital for nothing, provided Macquarie gave them the monopoly for the importation of 45,000 gallons of spirits during the following three years. Blaxcell and Riley knew little or nothing about building or hospitals, but their knowledge of the rum traffic was extensive.

Macquarie was rather dubious about the proposal, but his conscience was eased when the principal surgeon of the colony, D'Arcy Wentworth, became a party to the rum contract and so gave an ethical touch to the enterprise. The Governor gave his blessing to the hospital contract and eventually the building was erected in the street—the first straight street in Australia—named after His Excellency.

Conditions at Sydney Hospital during D'Arcy Wentworth's administration were revoltingly dreadful. There was no mortuary; the

15

kitchen was used when necessary as a 'dead house', and patients had to cook their own food in the wards. Rations were issued to every patient individually three times a week, so the wards were virtually a combination of scullery, kitchen and larder. No matter what the complaint or disease, every patient received the same rations of one pound of flour and one pound of meat. There were no vegetables, fruit, or milk.

Every evening at sundown the patients—they were mostly convicts—were mustered and locked in their wards until six o'clock the following morning, without any attendants or nurses to look after them. In the beginning there was no segregation of the sexes. No one thought cleanliness was important for the patients, so that it was not until thirty-four years after the hospital had been established that a bathroom was installed. It contained two baths for the entire hospital, and even then it was considered quite unnecessary.

With the advent of the bathroom came another novelty: an operating-theatre. Before that the surgeons did their operations in any part of the building, and there was no such thing as privacy. Visitors to the hospital would crowd round the surgeon while he was operating, often hindering his work. Needless to say, the medicos' methods were very crude. Before an amputation the lines of incision were marked out on the patient's body in ink with a quill pen. Ordinary sponges, never sterilised, where used, and after the amputation the wound was tied up with catgut. Nothing was sterilised; dressings usually comprised a kind of coarse hemp soaked in olive oil. Sometimes the patients recovered, if they were exceptionally lucky; usually septicaemia or gangrene set in and finished them off. All classes of diseases and complaints were admitted, although little or no effort at classification was made and treatment was practically nil. Cupping or blood-letting was the usual remedy.

James Bowman succeeded D'Arcy Wentworth in administering Sydney Hospital, and he secured some measure of order. Wardsmen were required to sleep on the premises, and Bowman himself made a daily inspection of the patients. Nevertheless, the surgeons were a troublesome enigma. Of medical officer Henry St John Younge, Governor Macquarie complained that he 'is by no means a desirable Acquisition in the Line of his Profession. He is exceedingly Ignorant as a medical man, being almost destitute of common Understanding and very low and Vulgar in Manners.' Surgeon Luttrell, who originally came to the colony as a farmer, was described by Macquarie as totally deficient 'in Attention to his Duty in regard to the unfortunate Persons placed under his care... he is sordid and unfeeling and will not Afford any medical assistance to any Person who cannot pay him well for it'. Shades of the Hippocratic oath!

It was difficult to get medical men for the colony, and how some of those engaged received their medical training is mystifying. When eventually orderlies were attached to the hospital, they were chosen at random from among the convicts, those useless for other work generally getting the jobs. The orderlies stole food and belongings from the patients, visitors stole anything they could lay their hands on, and those patients capable of leaving their beds stole from one another. When separate wards for men and women eventuated, a constable was stationed at the entrance to the women's ward to keep the men out. But he could not be there all the time and in any case was open to a bit of bribery to augment his meagre allowance.

Coming to more recent times, it may be added that nurses did not make their appearance in Sydney Hospital until the late 1860s when Sir Henry Parkes enlisted the aid of Florence Nightingale, who sent suggestions and recommendations for the training of nurses. In 1868 Miss Lucy Osburn arrived from England with a staff of five nurses, but they were by no means received with acclaim. The medical profession objected to this newfangled idea of trained women trying to help patients, and very often the doctors hindered the work of the nurses by keeping them in ignorance of the condition of patients, or of impending operations.

Gradually, however, the existing prejudice against Miss Osburn and her band of workers was worn down, and largely through the work of these devoted women Sydney Hospital really started to get under way. The old Rum Hospital building itself was condemned, and the present one opened in 1894.

MATRIMONIAL MATTERS

The old Parramatta prison for women convicts was a curious marriage bureau. It was half prison, half barracks, housing the women convicts of the colony, where they were fed and clothed by the Government in return for spinning and weaving wool into clothing and blankets.

During the regimes of early governors well-behaved lags were encouraged to exchange their convict shackles for the shackles of matrimony by choosing a bride from 'the Factory'. The old wall which enclosed a portion of the Factory may still be seen at Parramatta, New South Wales, a silent reminder of a unique institution in Australia's early days.

For a little more detail on the procedure of wife selection we can do no better than refer to the evidence of a Mr Mudie, a settler who was examined before a committee of the English House of Commons. In the course of his evidence on the matter he said, 'If a master has a convict that he is anxious to keep, and whom he considers to be well-behaved, it is considered a great indulgence if he gives him permission to get a wife from the Factory; but the master must enter into an agreement with the Government to feed and support the woman, and the offspring, to prevent their being a burden on the Government.

'This being done, the man goes and obtains an order to the matron of the Factory for a wife. The women are turned out, and they all stand up as you would place so many soldiers, or so many cattle at a fair. The same sort of ceremony and the same mode occurs with a free man; for the settlers also go to the Factory to select a wife.

'The man goes up and looks at the women; and if he sees a lady that takes his fancy he makes a sign to her, and she steps to one side. Some of the women refuse and stand still, for they have no wish to be married; but this is very rare. Then, of course, they have some conversation together, and if the lady is not agreeable, or if the man does not fancy her from her conversation, she steps back into the line, and the same ceremony goes on with two or three more. I have known instances of men going to the Factory and having the pick of two hundred women without finding anyone to please them. But eventually they find someone to suit them, and then they get married.'

An examination of the files of Australia's first newspapers reveals a number of references to the sale of wives for cash or barter. The following is an extract from a newspaper dated 23rd October, 1803, about a husband who bartered his wife for six bushels of wheat and a prize pig:

'The man at Baulkham Hills, who lately cried down the credit of his wife, did so merely to raise her reputation and enhance her worth, as he was desirous, probably, of making the best of a bad bargain. He has since converted her into an article of traffic, the net produce upon the sale of which amounted to six bushels of wheat and a large black inhabitant of the stye, received from a settler at Hawkesbury.'

Sales of wives, public and private, were common everyday affairs. One lady, who evidently possessed more than her share of glamour, brought for her better half no less than fifty sheep. Another wench was exchanged for £5 cash and a gallon of rum; yet another for twenty sheep and a gallon of rum.

A miner on the Victorian goldfields in 1859 sold not only his wife but his family as well. Another miner who purchased a wife and family took the case to law, because the family feather mattress was not included. The document, which was filed at the Bendigo Court, is still preserved. It has the miner's signature agreeing to the sale of his wife and children for £1.

Apart from the selling of wives, it seems that marriages could be dissolved simply by putting an advertisement to that effect in the local newspaper. A formula existed, beginning, 'A mutual separation having this day been entered into between me and my wife. . . .'

This advertisement appeared in an issue of December 1818: NOTICE. Whereas my wife, Jane ——, is again walked away with herself, without any provocation whatever, and, I hear, has taken up with a fellow who looked after cattle in the neighbourhood of Macquarie River. This is to give notice that I will not pay for bite nor sup, or for any other thing she may contract on my account to man or mortal; and that I am determined to prosecute with the utmost rigour the Law will permit, any person or persons who may harbour, conceal, or maintain the said runaway Jane ——after the publication of this advertisement.'

The *Derwent Star*, of Hobart, had a spicy style all its own in recording marriages. This appeared in an issue of 1810: ' MARRIAGE. On Monday, 26th ultimo, R. C. B——to Elizabeth T——, both late of Norfolk Island. They had cohabitated together for 14 years, verifying the old adage better late than never.'

Melbourne's first printed newspaper, the *Port Phillip Gazette*, contains many curious advertisements from wife-seeking bachelors. For instance, this on 28th August, 1839: 'MERI RIVER, WARRNAMBOOL. I, Henry Hull, overseer, hereby advertise for a wife. For preference a newly-arrived one, from 24 to 30 years of age. I am worth £80 ready cash and I do not mind if the woman has not got one pound. I will pay all her expenses to Warrnambool, and the sooner I get her the better.'

In the same newspaper two bachelors, in the one advertisement, set out their requirements and then wound up with this lyrical flourish: 'We express the pious hope that no prudish fears will withhold the ladies from answering this appeal to Cupid, but that they will joyously come forth in all their pristine purity to meet halfway those who will be but too happy to link their fates together in the bonds of holy matrimony.'

With such a shortage of ladies it's most surprising to see in the same matrimonial column this advertisement: 'Gentleman desires wife possessing £300. She must be tall and well-proportioned in every respect. Above all, a lady with small feet and well-turned ankles, expressive languishing blue eyes, good teeth and pouting lips.' One can't help wondering what luck this rather exacting gentleman met with.

BAKED HEADS FROM NEW ZEALAND

A highly profitable business for Sydney traders in the 1830s was the importation of tattooed Maori heads. An examination of the New South Wales Customs returns for those years will show among the list of items on which duty was payable—BAKED HEADS FROM NEW ZEALAND. Down George Street or adjoining streets in Sydney Town, the windows of several shops displayed these gruesome objects for sale. Or street pedlars—probably seamen—offered smuggled heads at a cheaper rate than those sold in the shops.

Prices for Maori heads in the shops generally ranged from one to two guineas, according to the amount of tattooing on them, but all were well baked and neatly stuffed with flax. The tattoo designs depicted a man's family background and prowess in battle; thus the higher a Maori was on the social scale and the more battles he survived, the more his face was tattooed.

Behind this once popular sale of Maori heads lies one of the many tragic aspects of the impact of European civilisation on a native Pacific people. One of the first Europeans to record a vigorous moral protest against this exploitation of traditional art for commercial gain was the Reverend Samuel Marsden, who visited New Zealand as a missionary. 'When I first came across this barbaric business,' he wrote, 'I recoiled in horror and disgust. Soon after my arrival in New Zealand a well-meaning native offered to collect a few samples for me. I told him and the other Maoris present that, if anyone dared to mention such a vile proposal in my presence again, I would see that the offender was immediately charged with murder. The Maoris were astonished at my attitude. They believed that I, like all the other white men who visited them, came only for the purpose of head-hunting.' Traders visiting New Zealand offered knives, tomahawks, and other such goods the Maoris coveted, in exchange for the heads of their enemies. Later, the Maoris were willing to supply heads only for muskets, and eventually when their consciences began to trouble them they refused to part with any more heads.

This change of attitude did not suit the owners of the trading vessels visiting New Zealand. Some of the more infamous of the traders turned head-hunters themselves and massacred tribes of Maoris to obtain their heads. One of these culprits was Captain Stewart of the brig *Elizabeth*, who figured in the massacre of five hundred Maoris to clinch a trading deal. In its later stages head-sellers sometimes paraded their living victims before a buyer and undertook to decapitate any heads selected, and even have the heads tattooed to order before decapitation.

Major-General H. G. Roberts, the hero of the Maori Wars, became so interested in the heads of his enemies that he published a hook on the subject. He gave details, with his own illustrations, on how to bake, clean and dry the heads most efficiently. One chapter explained the meaning of the various tattoo designs.

After some years of this gruesome trading in baked Maori heads, Governor Darling of New South Wales decided that it must stop. A proclamation was issued, and the new ruling was printed on the front page of the *Sydney Gazette* and also in the *Monitor*:

GOVERNMENT NOTICE

Colonial Secretary's Office,
Sydney, 16th April, 1831.

WHEREAS it has been represented to his Excellency the Governor that the masters and crews of vessels trading between this Colony and New Zealand, are in the practice of purchasing and bringing from thence human heads, which are preserved in a manner peculiar to that country: And whereas there is strong reason to believe, that such disgusting traffic tends greatly to increase the sacrifice of human life among savages whose disregard of it is notorious, his Excellency is desirous of evincing his entire disapprobation of the practice above-mentioned, as well as his determination to check it by all the means in his power, and with this in view, his Excellency has been pleased to order, that the Officers of the Customs do strictly watch and report every instance which they may discover of an attempt to import into the Colony any dried or preserved human heads in future, with the names of all parties concerned in every such attempt.

His Excellency trusts that to put a total stop to this traffic, it is necessary for him only thus to point out the almost certain and dreadful consequences which may be expected to ensue from a continuance of it, and the scandal and prejudice which it cannot fail to raise against the name and character of British Traders, in a country with which it is now become highly important for the merchants and traders of this Colony, at least, to cultivate feelings of natural goodwill; but if his Excellency should be disappointed in this reasonable expectation, he will feel it an imperative duty to take strong measures for totally suppressing the inhuman and very mischievous traffic in question.

His Excellency further trusts that all persons who have in their possession human heads recently brought from New Zealand, and particularly by the schooner *Prince of Denmark*, will immediately deliver them for the purpose of being restored to the relatives of the deceased parties to whom the heads belonged; this being the only possible reparation that can be rendered, and application having been specially made to his Excellency to the purpose.

By His Excellency's Command,
ALEXANDER M'LEAY

If tattooed Maori heads no longer grace the mantelpieces and walls of homes, there are many still to be seen in the museums of Europe. Incidentally, in the year 1896 a group of Maori visitors to the Canterbury Museum in Christchurch, New Zealand, saw the head of one of their family displayed in a glass case. They laid a complaint before the Dominion Governor and as a result the museum curator, Sir Julius Von Haast, was told to put the offending exhibit out of sight or take the consequences.

CURIOUS CLUBS

A droll organisation that flourished in Sydney in the 1890s was the outcome of a Shakespearian craze that had gripped the city. Its membership was large and representative; they called themselves the Society for Being Very Tired of Shakespeare. This was fairly typical of a number of curious clubs and odd organisations that sprang up in Australia toward the close of the nineteenth century. Among them

were the Bloomers Club, the Hot Potato Club, the Mutual Imps, and the Women Haters' Club.

The Bloomers Club was formed by a group of Melbourne women in the days when ardent feminists were attempting to introduce what they called 'rational costume'. The sensation it caused! Even the newspapers were shocked. The *Australasian*, in reporting a picnic held by members of the Bloomers Club, described the ladies' breeches as 'distinct cylinders', but blushingly admitted that after the picnic the ladies thought it prudent to conceal their new garments of freedom beneath conventional skirts. A Melbourne journal, the *Review of Reviews*, said it would not be surprising with such an unladylike craze if members of the Bloomers Club did not even discover a taste for smoking cigarettes.

The Fraternity of Mutual Imps was a society for men only. Its headquarters were in Melbourne, with branches in other capitals. Although its declared aim was to further the interests of art and literature, most of the members were more interested in corkscrew culture. The officials of the Fraternity of Mutual Imps were described as the arch fiend, past arch fiend, mutual fiends, and so on. Many distinguished citizens were among the fiends: artists, musicians, poets, actors, barristers. Theatrical members included J. C. Williamson, George Rignold, and Bland Holt. What became of this strange movement? Apparently it went the way of wax fruit and antimacassars.

Sydney's Hot Potato Club originated in the 1880s. All the members lived in Manly. The only night ferry left the city at 11.15 pm, and passenger club members made a practice of roasting potatoes in the engine furnaces.

The Western Australian goldfields saw the birth of the Women Haters' Club. A band of prospectors, embittered for many and varied reasons against females in general, got together and soothed their grievances by solemnly founding the organisation. Their self-imposed rules barred them from dealing with any store or pub that even employed female labour. Members of this club boasted that their hundred per cent masculine camp was the best conducted and the most efficient on the goldfields. Certainly, according to observers, it was one of the cleanest and neatest, even down to the cooking and washing.

These hefty miners took their club vows so seriously that when one of their numbers was injured, or suffered illness, a mate would stay in camp to nurse him—rather than let a woman do the job. When in due course a number of members left the field, this Women Haters' Club was broken up, but another Women Haters' Club was founded in 1902 in Dromana, Victoria.

SOUTH OF SYDNEY TOWN

The history of most Australian cities and towns is thick with colour and atmosphere. The thriving and progressive city of Wollongong is a far cry from its early beginnings. One of the difficulties of life in that centre in the early days was the water supply. A newspaper correspondent from Sydney, writing in 1847, gave Sydney readers a sidelight on it: 'Wollongong is anything but a well-watered township. In order to procure good water the people must go a distance of more than three miles. On one occasion I observed a tradesman there indulging in a libation resembling soup. When I inquired whether it was his usual practice to quench his thirst with soup he replied, to my astonishment, that it was not soup he was drinking but Wollongong water!'

The town of Wollongong can claim to have the first bathing machine built in Australia. Ten feet long, five and a half feet wide, and fitted with seats, the bathing machine was launched at Wollongong on 5th January, 1857, and was named the Mermaid. Single baths cost one shilling each. However, it was solely for the use of the ladies. And that brings us to a spot of scandal in regard to its purpose, as witness this extract from the local newspaper: 'The Mermaid—the new bathing machine at Wollongong—is the subject of many complaints. Well-dressed blackguards try to catch a glimpse of the ladies bathing there, and only retire reluctantly when requested to do so. Such conduct is unmanly and despicable, and ought to be severely punished.'

Exciting is the background of the New South Wales city of Goulburn. Goulburn's history includes many typical episodes of the roaring colonial days. A visitor to the town in 1833, after extolling its fine buildings and general air of prosperity, mentioned that the most conspicuous objects to be seen there were the gibbet and gallows on clear rising ground and visible to all. In those days executions were carried out in public, and practically all the townspeople would gather round to watch the hangings. In the 1830s two men were hanged for murder, and their bones were allowed to remain bleaching in the sun for months. It was only when the State Governor paid an official visit to Goulburn that the authorities, in having a general spring cleaning, cut down the skeletons and buried them.

The stations or farms around Goulburn used to employ large numbers of convicts. Periodically, a travelling magistrate accompanied by a trooper and a flogger would visit them and deal out 'justice' on the spot, and in no uncertain manner.

In the late 1840s poppies were extensively cultivated in Goulburn for the opium trade. Australia then had a fairly large Chinese population, and opium was much in demand.

One of the highlights of Goulburn's history was the 'dog war' of 1840. Stray dogs had become such a menace to the town that the police force instituted a campaign to round up all the mongrels and destroy them. The townspeople were asked to subscribe for a 'solid silver plate' to be given to the constable bagging the largest number of tails. It is recorded that one policeman was caught by the nose by one of the hounds, and another was bitten in a certain part of his anatomy which the official records described as 'a vulnerable spot'.

Today the city of Goulburn possesses little more than a dozen hotels; in the old days it boasted seventy-four. Of course in those times the inns played a much more important part in the life of the community than today. Not only were dances, balls, concerts, and meetings held in them, but they were used for police-court proceedings and church services. However, heavy drinking was the rule rather than the exception.

A colonist, writing in 1852, described a method practised in Goulburn for curing drunkenness. The patient was required to drink a quart of warm water containing a wineglassful of spirits and five grains of tartar emetic every morning. He was then carried to a dark room in the centre of which there was a large drum, on which he was fastened. The drum was then revolved rapidly. This treatment made the patient violently sick, whereupon he was soused with water and put to bed. Long before the probationary period had expired, the smell of spirits made him disgusted, and thus brought about his reformation.

Goulburn's famous jail had its exciting moments. There was the occasion when a prisoner employed in the tailor's shop making warders' uniforms planned an escape. One afternoon he rode up to the main gates dressed as a warder, with a long moustache, which he had made out of one of the jail brushes, carefully waxed at the ends. However, he was unlucky enough to meet the governor of the jail talking to some warders, whose suspicions were aroused; they tore off his false moustache and escorted him back to prison.

THE ROARING NINETIES

One time I spoke to a fine old pioneer who knew the Western Australian goldmining towns of Coolgardie and Kalgoorlie in their infancy. Among the stories he told me of those districts were these amusing ones.

'A well-known character in the early days of Kalgoorlie was an enterprising American who opened the first silent picture-show there.

28

It was so popular that a programme was shown every night of the week, including Sundays. The law didn't allow an admittance to be charged on Sundays, so the people were supposed to make a contribution of a silver coin before being admitted.

'As the threepenny bit was the smallest silver coin, most of the customers, naturally, just put a "trey" on the collection plate. But the shrewd Yankee proprietor soon found a way of defeating his cheap customers; he held on to all the trey bits that were given in, instead of paying them into the bank. Soon there was a shortage of that handy coin, and those who attended the show were forced to give sixpence. The picture-show bloke wasn't the only one to benefit; the clergy were greatly surprised to notice the greater value of the coins in their collection plates! Yes, the joke lasted a few months before the bank woke up.

'And I must tell you this incident about Coolgardie. When I first arrived there, water was scarce—damned scarce. After getting accommodation at a pub, I asked if I could have a bath. I was told I could have a shower, if that would do. "You bet," said I, so I crossed the yard to the bath-house. It was a rough affair, made from hessian bags. After I had undressed, I looked up to see what kind of a shower arrangement it was. Well, you can imagine the shock I got when I heard a harsh female voice call out, "Move a bit further over, Mr Wilkinson, so I can get the lot over you!" Standing on a platform, just over my head, was the burly form of Mrs Doyle, the licensee of the pub, with a large watering can in her hand!'

Even today in Coolgardie you can see reminders of the days when water was often more precious than gold. Half-buried piles of stones and decaying heaps of ashes scattered over the surface of every salt lake there are relics of the grim water shortage. With the influx of the pioneer miners the population of Coolgardie increased considerably, and the water position became alarming. The goldfields warden, realising the seriousness of the situation, posted up a notice warning the miners to leave the field as soon as possible. The warning had little effect. Men who had battled their way out of many tight corners wouldn't give up while there might still be a chance.

It was then that the salt lakes saved the day. One of the miners decided to construct a condenser, using a five-gallon oil drum as a boiler. The cooling process was a length of pipe made from empty jam tins, soldered together after the ends had been removed. Although the crude apparatus was small and required many hours' firing to produce enough water for the owner's daily requirements, it showed what could be done. Quickly other miners began copying the idea.

A scarcity of materials for making the condensing plants was a problem, but the miners were masters of makeshift. A few square iron tanks purchased from the teamsters, who carried water in them for their teams over the long dry stages, were used for boilers, and a few dilapidated sheets of corrugated iron were converted into lengths of pipe to cool the steam. Even the lack of tools did not daunt those pioneers. They made a soldering iron by melting a number of copper coins, pennies and halfpennies, into a mass and hammering it into shape. For solder they used the thousands of empty meat tins scattered over the camps. The tins were burnt in an open fire and the ashes dry-blown.

Many different types of boilers were tried, but the common square iron tank of two or four hundred gallons proved the most reliable, and was mostly used. It was simple to erect, easily cleaned, and not too expensive.

Most of the salt lakes appear to be dry, and people have asked if salt water was always available for condensing. In the beginning the miners often had to cart the salt water from those lakes, maybe many miles away, that contained water. As the mines developed, large quantities of salt water were found underground at various depths. The condensers played a great part in the development of the field. Many goldmining leases abandoned through the uncertainty of water were repegged, and miners, with the dread of a water famine removed, went to work with more confidence.

Before the invention of the condensers an incident occurred at Coolgardie that illustrates the hardships caused by the scarcity of water. A miner and his mate were in such dire straits that one of them pulled off his flannel shirt and placed it over a billy of boiling salt water to collect the steam. He wrung out the shirt into a dish, and so obtained sufficient water to save his own life and that of his mate.

They were the days of the Roaring Nineties, when most of Australia's male population headed for the Golden West. Ships put in at Albany because no harbour existed at Fremantle. On the way to the diggings of Coolgardie prospectors would pass the dry salt lakes, with their remarkable mirage that from a distance resembled water. The mirage broke the hearts of many, and others perished on the edges of those same waterless lagoons.

During the awful trek most men carried their worldly possessions and tucker on their backs. Others had all sorts of contrivances—prams, pushcarts, barrows, bikes, and other quaint structures on wheels—but never a horse. Some of the early comers had tried horses, but the bones of these poor animals lay along the sandy track to show that none could possibly survive without food and water in this kind of country. By the wayside, also, lay abandoned bicycles and carts, their skeletons telling a miserable story.

It was from Southern Cross that the majority of prospectors began their walk of three hundred miles to Coolgardie. A day or two out from the Cross they would pass the famous gum-tree, upon the trunk of which was roughly cut this notice:

> *Damn Coolgardie,*
> *Damn the track,*
> *Damn the road both there and back.*
> *Damn the water,*
> *Damn the weather,*
> *Damn Coolgardie altogether.*

Today, of course, those things are but memories, and Coolgardie is served with one of the finest water schemes in the country. It began with one of the most ambitious engineering projects of the 1890s, the scheme by which water was pumped 351 miles from Mundaring Weir in the Darling Range to Coolgardie. The scheme in its original state cost nearly £3 million, a prodigious sum in those days.

COBB AND CO

In its heyday Cobb and Co. was the largest single transport system in the world, with 20,000 horses in its stables. Cobb's coaches not only blazed a trail but made history and amassed a fortune for their founders.

When gold was first discovered at Ballarat, in Victoria, in 1851, the news spread to every country. Many gold-diggers in California, as well as men in other lands with no experience in searching for the elusive metal, decided to come to Victoria and try their luck on the new fields. Freeman Cobb, a young American coach-driver for the Adams and Co. Express in California, was one who arrived in Melbourne in 1852 to seek for gold.

Filled with enthusiasm, Cobb stepped ashore from the sailing vessel and pushed his way through the seething crowds of men of many nationalities, all preparing to make their fortunes. Impatiently he searched for a way of travelling to the goldfields without delay, but found the means of conveyance to be extremely primitive. Four alternatives were provided: people could travel by horse, by foot, by bullock teams, or by drays—loaded with boxes and casks—which bumped precariously over rough roads and arrived by good luck rather than the skill of the driver. To be sure, coach services operated in various parts of Australia, but none on the incredibly rough route to the Victorian goldfields.

With an unfailing business instinct Freeman Cobb realised that a bigger fortune could be made with a fast, reliable transport system from Melbourne to Ballarat than ever could be obtained on the goldfields there. The coaches would need to be specially sprung and the bodywork extra strong for the route they would traverse, and they would need to be driven by skilled drivers. Cobb saw the possibility of repeating in this new land what the coaching company had done in California. Returning to his homeland, the young man persuaded his former employers to help finance him with vehicles and experienced American coach-drivers; the folly of relying on local drivers was apparent, with the minds of all Victorians unhinged with thoughts of gold and men deserting their employment for the diggings.

Freeman Cobb formed a company of four Americans with a com-

bined capital of £23,000, and within seven days of the first of the American coaches to be landed at the Port of Melbourne a regular service was established on the Geelong route. With the arrival of more coachlines and their Californian drivers the main goldfield towns of Ballarat, Bendigo, and Castlemaine were served by Cobb and Co. Gradually Australian drivers with sound bush knowledge worked with the American drivers and became skilled, hardy coachmen.

Two years after launching his business, Freeman Cobb, now a wealthy young man, left it and travelled to the United States with his fortune, leaving behind a name used as a trade name that became headlines in the journal of Australian history. After his departure Cobb and Co. continued its activities until 1861, when another American, James Rutherford, bought out its two owners. It was Rutherford (he had come to Victoria as a goldseeker on the same ship as Freeman Cobb) who really built up and expanded Cobb and Co. to every State in Australia, and whose genius for organising and administrating produced the greatest firm of coach proprietors this country has ever known. Rutherford once told of the occasion when he saw the first Cobb and Co. coach. At the time he was a twenty-five-year-old digger with spade, pick and washpan, on his way to the goldfields. He stood aside to let the coach pass, and as he looked at the receding vehicle he had the strange impression that he saw a rainbow above it. If he did, it was a rainbow that led him to reach riches much greater than those amassed by the original founder of Cobb and Co.

Rutherford ceased importing American coaches and established the company's own coachbuilding firm in Ballarat. Here was built the largest coach ever seen in Australia and quite possibly the whole world. It was named the Leviathan, and was built to seat eighty-two passengers in comfort, but on occasions it carried a hundred persons travelling inside and outside. Twenty-two horses running in pairs were harnessed to the huge vehicle, and four postillions, in addition to the driver, were required to manage the long team. The coach itself was twenty-five feet in length and had plate-glass windows. The famous coach-painter Ned Chester was commissioned to paint and decorate it.

After the coming of the railways to Ballarat the great coach was transferred to another Victorian route; then it was sent to service in the Deniliquin to Hay run in New South Wales. Still retreating farther west, it went to Adelaide and was used on the Adelaide to Glenelg road. Finally, in 1900, it was taken to Western Australia to begin a service on the Coolgardie goldfield. What became of it after that is a mystery. Not even the people of Coolgardie, or members of the Western Australian Historical Society, can trace the end of the Leviathan.

Cobb's and Rutherford's slogan was 'Follow the Gold'. This policy brought them business, and business brought them riches. In the first five gold years 240,000 people landed in Melbourne, and nearly all the newcomers tried the goldfields. They were restless and moved from place to place seeking wealth. Cobb and Co. was their main means of transport. Apart from the passengers carried, the company secured a monopoly of mail contracts and so was assured of a lucrative income from the Government.

There was little danger of Cobb and Co. coachmen deserting their employers for the lure of the goldfields. They were paid wages which appeared fabulous for those times: unheard-of pay packets of £1,000 a year with free meals and accommodation at the coaching hotels.

When a coach came to a very steep hill, the driver would pull up and insert steel shoes or turned-up plates under the wheels; they were attached to the coach by means of stout chains. The coach would then skid down: very simple and effective, especially when the coach had a full load. This procedure gave the passengers added confidence, since they knew that the driver was not relying entirely on his brakes. Reaching the bottom, the coach would again be stopped, the shoes withdrawn and the journey resumed.

As already mentioned, Cobb and Co. were not the pioneers of coaching in Australia. Long before the company came from Victoria to make its New South Wales headquarters at Bathurst, in 1862, there were many coach services throughout the colony. One famous owner and coach-driver was Bill Maloney, who serviced the prosperous mining towns of Hill End, Sofala, and Tambaroora from Bathurst. Immensely popular with travellers, Bill naturally resented the advent of the mighty competitor from Victoria with its large coaches equipped for faster and more comfortable transport. He voiced his disapproval in the ditty he sang when he drove his five-horse team.

> *Now look here, Cobb and Co,*
> *A lesson take from me.*
> *If you meet me on the road*
> *Don't you make too free.*
> *For if you do you'll surely rue...*
> *You think you do it fine,*
> *But I'm a tip-and-slasher*
> *Of the Tambaroora line.*

I can hold them, steer them
   And drive them to and fro...
With ribbons well in hand, me bhoys,
   I can make 'em go.
With me foot well on the brake, lads,
   I'm bound to make them shine,
For I'm a tip-and-slasher
   Of the Tambaroora line.

Always he shouted the words as he saw a Cobb and Co. coach approaching, or whenever he overtook one of them (as he invariably did) on the narrow, winding road between Bathurst and Hill End. The Cobb and Co. driver would take no risk on this nightmare road, but Bill Maloney fearlessly drove his coach along it almost at a gallop.

It was the policy of the ever expanding organisation of Cobb and Co. to buy out their competitors, paying full value for coaches and equipment plus generous compensation for the goodwill of the business. But no money would buy out Bill Maloney, and, despite his rival's better-equipped vehicles and the amenities the company offered to passengers, his customers stuck to him.

It was a day of triumph for the Irishman when Cobb and Co. decided to relinquish its coach service round the Bathurst district. Before leaving, James Rutherford invited Maloney to inspect his factory to see the coaches being built for all over Australia and New Zealand. He showed him one particularly fine vehicle which happened to be painted in the colours Bill always used and which was equipped with five sets of the very best of harness.

'What do you think of this outfit, Bill?' asked Rutherford. 'Would you be interested in it?'

Bill looked longingly at the coach, noting every detail of its superb craftsmanship. 'It's a beauty,' he replied, 'but I couldn't afford a job like that.'

Rutherford smiled and placed his hand on Maloney's shoulder. 'I'm giving it to you as a gift, Bill. I want to show my appreciation of you for being such a clean rival on the roads. It should set you up for life.'

Rutherford's prediction was certainly fulfilled, for Maloney continued to run coaches on the Tambaroora line, with his son Bill to help him and to continue the line after his father died at a great age.

Cobb and Co. serviced not only every State in Australia, but other countries as well: New Zealand, South Africa, and Japan. The latter country was its only failure. A team of coaches was taken to Japan and passenger and freight services were commenced, but the wily Japanese started opposition lines, built coaches in imitation of Cobb's, cut the fares, and quickly undermined the Australian firm.

The coming of the railways sounded the death-knell of Cobb and Co. It is significant that their coaches never ran in Sydney or Brisbane, for the railways took over at various points. Many city people had never seen a Cobb's coach except in pictures. Until the late 1940s there was in existence a Cobb and Co's Old Coach Drivers' Association, including as its members former employees not only in Australia, but also in New Zealand.

James Rutherford never returned to America. He took a close interest in the town of Bathurst, became its mayor for a period, and was for thirty years treasurer to the Agricultural Society. He beautified Bathurst with tree-planting, and exercised an open-handed philanthropy. During his long governing directorship of Cobb and Co. he acquired several pastoral properties in New South Wales and Queensland, and even in his eighties he continued to supervise them. He was on a visit to one of his properties when he died at Mackay, Queensland, in 1911.

Two notable poets, Henry Lawson and Will Ogilvie, have paid tribute to Cobb and Co. Lawson wrote in 'The Lights of Cobb and Co':

> *The roaring camps of Gulgong, and many a 'Digger's Rest',*
> *The diggers on the Lachlan; the huts of the Farthest West;*
> *Some twenty-thousand exiles who sailed for weal or woe,*
> *The bravest hearts of twenty lands will wait for Cobb and Co.*
> *Past haunted half-way houses—where convicts made the bricks—*
> *Scrub-yards and new bark shanties, we dash with five and six;*
> *Through stringybark and blue-gum, and box and pines we go—*
> *A hundred miles shall see tonight the lights of Cobb and Co!*

WOES OF THE EARLY GOVERNORS

The powers possessed by the early New South Wales Governors have been unequalled in the history of the British Dominions. Until 1824 there was no restraining Council influence or legal adviser, and the authority of these Governors was absolute. (The Imperial Government omitted to make definite legal provision for the civil government of the colony, consequently many of the orders and regulations of the early Governors were invalid.) They could—and they did—condemn, execute or reprieve at will, allot grants of land or refuse them, and there was no appeal. 'The law, sir? I am the law!' is an oft-quoted remark of Governor Bligh. Still, no one would envy these rulers; their worries were legion.

Macquarie wrote on his arrival in Sydney: 'I found the colony barely emerging from infantile imbecility, and suffering from various privations and disabilities; the country impenetrable beyond forty miles from Sydney; agriculture in a yet languishing state; commerce in its early dawn; revenue unknown; threatened with famine; distracted by faction; the public buildings in a state of dilapidation and mouldering on decay; the few roads and bridges formerly constructed rendered almost impassable; no public credit nor private confidence; the morals of the great mass of the population in the lowest state of debasement, and religious worship almost wholly neglected.' He also said that the colony consisted of 'those who had been transported, and those who ought to have been'.

Macquarie set about correcting the immorality, drunkenness and criminality he found in his seat of government, for, as he had indicated, the Sydney of that day was wild and lawless. Respectability was almost non-existent—it was a rarity for couples to bother about going through a marriage ceremony and the bulk of the population got drunk habitually. Robberies and violent assaults were commonplace. The new Governor created a civil police force and divided the town into five districts, each with its watch-house and lock-up. The constabulary numbered about forty members and each was equipped with a Navy cutlass and a watchman's rattle. A few ex-soldiers and sailors were included in the force, but most of them were emancipated prisoners, and even convicts who were still actually serving sentences themselves.

In Van Diemen's Land the early Governors had their own troubles. Giving evidence before the English House of Commons on the moral conditions of the island, a speaker described Van Diemen's Land as 'that den of thieves, that cave of robbers, that cage of unclean birds, that isthmus between hell and earth. . .' Sales of wives were common, eligible *de factos* had been auctioned in the open market and, despite the fact that two people had actually married there in 1817, marriage was regarded as an old-fashioned custom that had been relegated to the past. Nevertheless, observance of the Sabbath was strictly commanded by law, and historian James Bonwick relates that 'Colonel Collins, first Lieutenant-Governor of Hobart Town, though not susceptible to religious emotion, not devoted to Church celebration, and not conspicuous for the ordinary virtues, was nevertheless sufficiently possessed of the instincts of an officer and a gentleman to observe the proprieties of Sunday service'.

This compulsory Sabbath observance resulted in excellent church congregations, but only numerically speaking. When the Rev. William Bedford pointed out to Governor Arthur that very few of the churchgoers were legally married, and the incongruity of preaching Sunday after Sunday to pews of Hobart's best known ladies of the town who had no intention of changing their profession, the Governor decided to do something about it. His solution was a simple one that would perhaps not be regarded today as particularly drastic, but it caused turmoil and frenzied panic as no other government order did before or since in Tasmania. Governor Arthur decreed that all government employees had to be married to the ladies they lived with.

To the uproar, the pleas, the threats and appeals, His Excellency turned a deaf ear. Respectability or dismissal was the implacable command. Since most of the ladies living in comfortable concubinage had graduated from the town jail, few of their gentlemen friends wished actually to marry them. Hence they were cast off to fend for themselves whilst their 'protectors' looked around for legal partners of a higher social standing.

As in New South Wales and Tasmania, the other Australian colonies were also trouble spots for their early Governors. Until he was eventually recalled, the governorship of Hindmarsh, South Aus-

41

tralia's first Governor, was marked by long and weary wrangling with the Resident Commissioner, Fisher, and Surveyor General Colonel Light. The latter had chosen the present site for the infant capital, but the Governor voiced his disapproval in no uncertain terms. There were a number of reasons why the proposed town should have been built nearer the sea, many of them perfectly logical, but Colonel William Light persisted in defiance of the Governor until Adelaide was laid along the banks of the River Torrens some six miles from the nearest point on the Gulf of St Vincent.

Victoria's first Governor, Charles La Trobe, had his share of woes. He even had to bring his own house with him from England. When he was commissioned he was advised that there was a serious shortage of dwellings in the colony, so he brought with him on the ship a weatherboard cottage in sections. That same building—Victoria's first Government House—is still preserved in Melbourne.

Governor La Trobe also brought out with him his Swiss wife. When the vessel arrived, a brave showing of flags and bunting greeted them and one or two decorated arches had been erected. Unfortunately, when the vice-regal pair stepped off the boat something went wrong with the gangway plank, and the Governor and his lady stepped nearly knee-deep into mud. Still in their muddy state they were escorted in triumph along the rough roads with their cheering and waving people; history is silent on any comment they may have made.

The concluding statement in the first report of Queensland's first Governor, Sir George Bowen, reads as follows: 'As to money wherewith to carry on Government, I started with just sevenpence halfpenny in the Treasury. A thief broke into the Treasury a few nights after my arrival and carried off the sevenpence halfpenny mentioned. However, I borrowed money from the banks until our revenue came in.'

The Iron Horse

The thirteenth day of September 1854 was a great day for Melbourne. From early morning a big crowd had been gathering in Flinders Street from the railway terminus down toward the wharf. Rich and poor, well-dressed and ragged, rubbed shoulders in an atmosphere of excitement the colony had never before known. There were flags

flying, gay bunting, a brass band playing lively airs, laughter and cheers.

It was a day to celebrate; for just beyond the terminus gates stood the Iron Horse—the great fire-breathing monster that was to make history for Melbourne. Australia's first train, indeed the first one in the Southern Hemisphere, was getting ready for its maiden run, from Flinders Street to Port Melbourne. Yes, it was a great day for Melbourne and a slap in the eye for her rival, Sydney.

The Melbourne *Argus* was very dignified about the whole affair. Thus it reported:

'Three carriages were in attendance for the conveyance of guests. They were handsomely painted and varnished, and very commodious. But the locomotive attracted more of the attention of the crowds; it is six-wheeled with a tubular boiler, and the tender is on the same body as the engine. Its power of traction is equal to 130 tons at the speed of 25 miles an hour.

'Shortly after 12 o'clock, His Excellency the Lieutenant Governor, Sir Charles Hotham, accompanied by Lady Hotham, arrived at the station. His Excellency was presented with copies of the by-laws and the timetable, printed upon satin. Sir Charles and Lady Hotham were then conducted to one of the carriages, and all three carriages were speedily laden with their full complement. An open carriage, next to the locomotive, contained the band of the 40th Regiment. Australia's first train started at twenty minutes past twelve to the music of the band and the cheering, clapping, and waving of hats of the vast crowd of spectators.'

No wonder that Sydney was green with jealousy now that Melbourne possessed the first and only railway in Australia. Sydney newspapers grudgingly gave a little space in their columns to the account of the great event as sent to them by the *Argus*. However, one Sydney newspaper, the *Empire*, happened to have a representative on the spot. He added this epilogue to the report:

'Without wishing in the least to disparage the important event, as reported by the Melbourne *Argus*, I will present you with the actual facts.

'Sir Charles and Lady Hotham and a considerable number of distinguished citizens having taken their places in the train, the signal was given to proceed. The steam was turned on, a whistle shrieked, but the Iron Horse would not budge an inch. Great was the dismay on the faces of the engineer and engine-driver. The valve was opened to its widest extent, and the pantings of the overladen steam horse were quite alarming.

'The regimental band struck up a lively tune to hide the utter confusion, but still the train refused to move. A whole host of railway porters and policemen set to work and pushed the train along the line by main force for a hundred yards. It was useless.

'More police then came. Directors of the railway company—stout gentlemen in top-hats and dress-suits, ready for the celebration banquet—applied shoulders vigorously to the buffer of the last carriage. At last, by slow degrees, the train moved amid shouts of laughter from the assembled thousands in Flinders Street.

'With great exertion the train was pushed on to the wooden bridge that crosses the Yarra. Here, the gradient being easier, the train slowly got into motion and went away at the rate of 15 miles an hour.'

Maybe the Sydney reporter exaggerated a little, maybe not. At any rate Sydney recovered some of its lost face and openly sniggered and scoffed at this anticlimax. Nothing, however, could alter the fact that her rival had beaten her in the march of progress, and it was five years before Sydney could boast of a similar undertaking.

TRAMWAY TOPICS

A woman approaches a tram terminus in Sydney. A conductor steps down from his tram to meet her and, with courtly grace, shakes hands with the woman and helps her aboard.

'Thank you, conductor.'

'Please take a seat, madam. But first let me dust it.'

'Thank you. And would you tell the driver to be very careful. I just can't abide this newfangled craze for fast travelling.'

'Leave it to me, madam. Now are all passengers comfortably seated?' There is a chorus of assent. 'Very good. Then off we go!'

Believe it or not, that was a typical scene in the days of Sydney's steam trams during the late 1880s. If you are sceptical, here are some of the rules from the list of official regulations laid down for conductors:

The tram conductor must welcome and shake hands with all passengers, and conduct ladies to their seats.

He should dust each seat before the passenger sits on it.

The conductor must next inquire if everyone is comfortably seated. Then he should look right and left before signalling the driver to start.

On the route he must call out the names of all intersections, junctions, and the various stores.

Should the conductor notice any strangers in the tram, he should direct the attention of such passengers to places of scientific or historical interest.

At crossings the conductor must walk ahead of the tram with a red flag by day and a red lamp by night. He must also hold up cross traffic with a red flag and signal the tram to proceed by waving a green flag.

With the advent of the double-decker trams the conductors always carried string for the needs of the ladies. Southerly busters blew up ladies' skirts on the top of trams, and the string was a first-aid measure.

In the 1890s Sydney had the finest steam-tram system in the world. You could post your letters on the trams and be assured of an express mail delivery. The express trams from such outlying places as Bondi, Coogee, and La Perouse whisked you to work at fifty miles an hour non-stop! Slow, local steam trams were backed into sidings to let the express trams through. First- and second-class accommodation were provided on the express trams. Their crews were proud of their reputation for speed and schedule. Passengers stop-watched the drivers and laid bets on the morning race, such as the Bondi express beating the Woollahra one, or the La Perouse tram licking the Botany tram.

Taylor Square, Darlinghurst, and Mark Foy's corner were winning-posts. The pointsmen were exceedingly worried men when the express mails came hurtling from different directions to the intersection. Luckily there was never a dead heat.

It was during this period that Fishing Specials were introduced. These took fishermen by express steam tram to the old Bondi terminus near the top of Tamarama. Fishermen boarded the trams with their gear and spent a day on the rocks with rod and line. Kegs of beer were placed in a special truck attached to the tram. Beer and bait were bought from the drivers and conductors, who were keen fishermen themselves. Those unlucky enough not to catch any fish did not need to go home in disgrace; there was always plenty to buy from those who did make hauls, and you could buy a basket of mixed fish for a shilling.

Many of the drivers of the ordinary local steam trams had pets that accompanied them on their daily runs. Best known was Teddy, the two-up cockatoo who was an expert at heading the pennies with his beak. He was much in demand at the trammies' two-up school in the rocks at the foot of Waverley Bay.

Another of the pets was a hen who, on the daily run, rarely missed laying an egg for the heavily moustached driver. Then there was the rooster who always crowed when the tram reached the top of a hill. Possums, too, rode on the steam trams and in winter would huddle near the engine or even drape themselves on the drivers' necks. And many fine tom-cats were drivers' pets. They were sudden death to rats at Darlinghurst water siding.

On Sundays the trams always stopped for the church hour. Many a Sunday's dinner was warmed in front of the fire on the engine, and picknickers could get plenty of hot water—given with the best of goodwill—for their billy tea. Such was the friendliness and community spirit of those days that the drivers would often wash the children's dirty faces with warm engine water and a clean rag. And there was never a tram strike or stopwork meeting of protest.

When the tramway authorities in Sydney tried out an electric tram for the first time, there were no overhead wires; the power was in a storage battery on the tram. Also the lines were the ordinary ones on which the old steam trams ran. The experiment was unsuccessful, and after a trial of about two weeks the electric tram was taken off. However, a most interesting fact was the official reason for its discontinuance; the tramway department stated that the tram had proved a failure because the electricity affected the watches of passengers!

Trams have now vanished from the streets of Sydney, and buses have taken their place. The modern-day bus driver is of another race and, for that matter, so is the modern-day passenger.

YESTERYEARS

The First Rabbits; Pure Merinos; The Burke and Wills Tragedy;
The Sacred Nugget Goldrush; The First Lottery;
The Westralia Mine Rescue; The Magpie Professor; Show Business;
Art Surprises; A Poor Simple Fool.

THE FIRST RABBITS
Who brought the first rabbits to Australia? Here they are—the six guilty men: Governor Phillip, Governor King, John Pascoe Fawkner, a Bass Strait sealer (name unknown), Commander Stokes, and Thomas Austin. Of course, they would have been furious if anyone challenged the innocence of their actions in their own lifetime. They craved rabbit

meat as a change from monotonous mutton diet. They wanted rabbits to shoot for sport. They wanted the rabbits to keep as pets for their children. In their own eyes they were public benefactors.

If we were able to let those six guilty men speak for themselves, they might have something to say like this:

PHILLIP: I, Captain Phillip, am number one on your list of guilty men. Of the five little rabbits that came out to Australia with the First Fleet, I was the owner of three. The other two belonged to the Officers' Quarters. When we left England we had a considerable brood of rabbits aboard the Fleet to provide fresh meat for the soldiers. In those days scurvy was a deadlier peril than shipwreck. There were only five rabbits left at the end of the journey. Even so, they did not last long; just after our arrival in 1788 they were made into a rabbit pie for my table. Therefore, though manifestly the first man to bring the rabbit to Australia, I can hardly be held blameworthy for the subsequent spread of the pestilential little rodent from one end of the country to the other.

And you, Governor King?

KING: I am not as guilty as some people would paint me. My trouble, like Governor Phillip's, was also an understandable craving for rabbit pie. That is why I imported some edible specimens from Cape Town in 1791. Never in my lifetime did they take to the bush. Thirty-five years after I imported those specimens they were still being bred in hutches in Sydney. And they were regarded as rare delicacies.

Third guilty man is that dynamic man of Melbourne Town, John Pasch Fawkner.

FAWKNER: Man of Melbourne Town, indeed! I'll have you know, sir, that I was the founder of Melbourne, no matter what that fellow John Batman had to say to the contrary!

'This will be the place for a village,' said Batman. A village indeed! I chose the site for the future city. The whole of the pioneering job was left in my hands, and I did it well and truly. What is more, I lived to see Melbourne grow into the proudest city in the Southern Hemisphere.

I was the founder of Melbourne's first newspaper. I was the owner of Melbourne's first general store and hotel.

You were also the owner of Melbourne's first pair of rabbits.

FAWKNER: True, sir! And proud I am of that fact! Don't you dare lay the blame of any rabbit plague at my doorstep! My pair of rabbits never went bush. Good day, sir!

History does not record the name of the sealer in Bass Strait who was guilty man number four.

SEALER: I don't think my name matters in the least. But I've nothing to be ashamed about. In the year 1836 I liberated a pair of rabbits on an island off Wilson's Promontory. I understand that today it's known as Rabbit Island.

My idea was to provide fresh food for castaway sailors. Well, that happy pair multiplied so rapidly that six years later there was a colony of rabbits on the island numerous enough to feed an army corps. It may interest you to know that when Commander Stokes called at the island he placed on record the fact that I had done a most worthy act.

STOKES: Our friend speaks the truth. Incidentally, it was I, Commander Stokes, who named Rabbit Island from the abundance of rabbits I saw there. And, later, when I learnt that those animals multiplied from a single pair turned loose by that praiseworthy sealer, I was encouraged to emulate his example. For the benefit of any unfortunate voyagers who might be thrown hungry ashore in the locality of the Kent Group, I placed a pair of rabbits on one of the islands there.

I think we must all agree that it was a thoughtful act on the part of Commander Stokes. Nevertheless, he must be regarded as a guilty party. Number six was Thomas Austin, a prosperous landowner of Barwon Park, near Geelong, Victoria.

AUSTIN: Being an Englishman, I felt rather lonely in the Western District of Victoria, so it was with much enthusiasm that I imported twenty-four English wild rabbits. The year was 1859. I hoped to breed them in sufficient numbers to provide the sport of shooting for myself and my few neighbours. I longed to see my estate looking more like the English countryside with a few white tails bobbing about at eventime.

When the rabbits arrived, I caged them and succeeded in getting together a nice stock—still in cages. Then I built some warm shelters in the grounds, planted suitable grasses and clover close by, and carefully installed a few pairs of bunnies.

I wondered whether the outdoor life would suit them. I feared that they would not be able to fend for themselves, like sheep and cattle. It was, I thought, risky to expose the dear little furry creatures to the hazards of the Australian bush. Oh dear, I need not have worried! The result of the liberation was successful. Very successful. Encouraged by my tender nursing, they multiplied so rapidly that even the shooting did not diminish their numbers. Within six years, although we had killed off some twenty thousand, there were thousands more in full possession of my property.

Of the six men on trial, Thomas Austin was undoubtedly the guiltiest. Now it would take an astronomer to calculate the numbers of rabbits descended from his 1859 experiment. In twenty years the descendants of the Englishman's little flock numbered hundreds of millions. They swarmed over Victoria and New South Wales, stocked up Queensland and South Australia. By the end of the century they were marching to the west—2,000 miles on their way.

Until 1902, when the first rabbit was seen near Perth, Western Australians had believed that the barrier of 2,000 miles of desert country would be adequate to keep out the rabbit pest of the eastern States. Western Australia woke up in alarm, and got busy with wire netting to keep back the invasion.

A fence, they decided, would be built from ocean to ocean, from Starvation Bay on the Great Australian Bight to beyond Condon on the Indian Ocean: 1,200 miles of wire-netted rabbitproof fencing, 1,200 miles of one continuous straight line of fencing. But, as they feverishly erected this mighty barrier, it was realised that the rabbits were on both sides of it. Without hesitation another—a check fence—was commenced, 300 miles farther west. This was a mere 700 miles long. It was finished in nine weeks. Think of that for fast work; 80 miles a week over dry, roadless country where all material had to be transported on camel-back. I read in an overseas publication that Mexico claimed the world's record for a continuous line of fence: 100 miles on a cattle ranch. That should make even the rabbits laugh.

PURE MERINOS

In the 1830s, when Major-General Sir Richard Bourke, the Governor of New South Wales, was the well-beloved autocrat of the colony, had you, as a stranger, asked some Sydneyite to point out a 'Pure Merino' in the streets of the town, he would have stared at you in astonishment. Everybody knew who the Pure Merinos were, surely! They were by no means inconspicuous in the oddly mixed society of New South Wales as to be easily mistaken.

When he became assured that you were in earnest and quite guileless, he would begin to study the passers-by and presently might say, 'Well now, here comes Mr John Blaxland and Mr Gregory Blaxland, his brother. They, of course, are Pure Merinos. Oh, and there is Dr Wardell of Petersham, the friend of young Mr William Charles Wentworth—he's one, too. And see over there that distinguished-looking gentleman talking to the old parson? Those two are Mr justice Forbes and the Reverend Samuel Marsden of St John's. Very Pure Merinos they are!'

'I see. And those two clever-looking gentlemen talking together on the corner of the street, are they not Pure Merinos also?'

'Heaven forbid! No, not at all. They are Old Hands. Surely you know that? Emancipists.'

'Emancipists?'

'Yes, of course. They came out here as convicts. One of them, Dr Redfern, was mixed up in a shipboard mutiny. The other, old Dr Bland, fought a duel with a brother officer in the Navy in India and killed his opponent.'

'So emancipists are former convicts?'

'Yes, men who have once been, but no longer are, convicts. Some have served their full time, others have been fortunate enough to be granted an absolute or conditional pardon by the Governor. In any case, they are all known as emancipists. Those two doctors by the way, are well respected men here in Sydney Town, but everyone knows they are ex-convicts and could never be in the social class of the Pure Merinos.'

'But surely in the case of emancipists who are pre-eminently the mental superiors of most of their fellow citizens, they are entitled to every reward that success in life can offer?'

'It is easy to perceive, sir, that you are a total stranger to this country. Class distinction is rigidly observed in the colony of New South Wales. Emancipists are tolerated if their background warrants it. But, though some possess high education and others have become wealthy citizens, neither brains nor money can bridge the chasm that separates them from Pure Merinos. No, sir!'

Until Macquarie arrived as the new Governor of the colony, the emancipists remained outcasts, so far as social recognition went. Macquarie's idea was that the men who had become free should have every assistance in re-establishing themselves in society and should be eligible for appointment to any situation for which, by continued good conduct, they might have shown their worthiness.

Not long after his arrival he put this theory into practice. Emancipists were allowed to act as lawyers and magistrates, when they had the required qualifications, and to fill other public offices. There was an immediate uproar from the Pure Merinos. The first Supreme Court judge refused to let emancipist lawyers practise before him. Bitter quarrels began and as a result Governor Macquarie was recalled in 1821. His successor, Sir Thomas Brisbane, was instructed by the Colonial Office in London that, although Macquarie's principle was a right and just one, he should not excite the animosity of the blue bloods—the Pure Merinos—by forcing this principle upon them except in the most tactful manner.

THE BURKE AND WILLS TRAGEDY

A monument standing near Parliament House, Melbourne, nobly commemorates Robert O'Hara Burke, leader of the tragic Burke and Wills expedition, Victoria's first national undertaking and the pioneer exploration across the continent from south to north. Burke and Wills were brave men and the story of their great achievement forms a stirring chapter in the history of Australian exploration by land. Adam Lindsay Gordon has paid a worthy tribute in verse to Burke:

In Collins Street standeth a statue tall—
*   A statue tall on a pillar of stone,*
Telling its story, to great and small,
*   Of the dust reclaimed from the sand waste lone.*
Weary and wasted, and worn and wan,
*   Feeble and faint, and languid and low,*
He lay on the desert, a dying man,

*   Who has gone, my friends, where we all must go.*
With the pistol clenched in his failing hand,
*   With the death mist spread o'er his fading eyes,*
He saw the sun go down on the sand,
*   And he slept, and never saw it rise...*

Because of the disasters associated with it, the fact seems often forgotten that the expedition, or portion of it, was the first to cross Australia from south to north. On Monday, 20th August, 1860, a large crowd assembled on the outskirts of Melbourne to see the great cavalcade leave. The goodwill, the pride and enthusiasm of the people were manifest when it wound out of Royal Park, a seemingly endless procession of wagons, horses and camels, attended by bronzed white men and swarthy, brightly attired Sepoys from India. On this crisp winter morning there were no shadowy thoughts of possible tragedy, only bright visions of success and glory.

Four months after leaving

ROBERT O'HARA BURKE

Melbourne, the expedition reached Cooper's Creek. It had travelled 700 miles toward the shores of the Gulf of Carpentaria; ahead lay as many miles through trackless, unexplored country. Burke decided to

WILLIAM JOHN WILLS

form a depot at the Creek and push on with three others: Wills, King, and Gray. Their efforts were rewarded when, to their joy, the Gulf of Carpentaria was sighted.

Then began the return journey, south, with Gray a very sick man. A record of the perilous trek is contained in the diary kept throughout by Wills:

APRIL 17. Just as we were leaving camp, Gray died. He had not spoken a word since his first attack of illness. Poor

Gray must have suffered very much. The three of us are also very weak. It was with difficulty that we could dig a grave sufficiently deep to bury Gray ...

Four days later Burke, Wills and King, with two camels, reached Cooper's Creek at the place where the depot party had been established. To their horror there was no one there.

Our bitter disappointment may well be imagined. We arrived at the depot in the evening of *the very day the party started off for the Darling River.* They had left a note saying that their camels were well and in good condition. As our camels are done up, and were scarcely able to reach this depot we have very little chance of overtaking them. To think we should reach here exhausted, after four months of the severest travelling and privation, just a few hours after the depot party left! Our legs are almost paralysed. We find it a most trying task to walk only a few yards.

From under a tree marked with the words DIG. APRIL 21, 1861, we extracted the note and some provisions. Fortunately, this food should be sufficient to take us to the bounds of civilisation. Flour, 50-lbs; rice, 20-lbs; oatmeal, 60-lbs; sugar, 60-lbs; and dried meat, 15-lbs. These provisions, together with a few horseshoes and nails, constitute all the articles left. We are in a very awkward position as regards clothing.

Before the disappointed trio left Cooper's Creek, Burke wrote the following note and buried it in a box on the spot:

Depot No. 2, Cooper's Creek Camp 65. The return party from Carpentaria, consisting of myself, Wills and King (Gray dead) arrived here last night and found that the depot party had only started on the same day. We proceed on, tomorrow, slowly down the creek towards Adelaide by Mount Hopeless, and shall endeavour to follow Gregory's track; but we are very weak. The two camels are done up, and we shall not be able to travel faster than four or five miles a day. Gray died on the road, from exhaustion and fatigue. We have all suffered much from hunger. The provisions left here will, I think, restore our strength. We have discovered a practicable route to Carpentaria, the chief position of which lies in the 140 deg. of East Longitude. There is some good country between this and the Stony Desert. From thence to the tropics the land is dry and stony. Between the Carpentaria a considerable portion is rangy, but well watered and richly grassed. We reached the shores of Carpentaria on the 11th February, 1861. Greatly disappointed at finding the party here gone.

ROBERT O'HARA BURKE, Leader.

April 22, 1861.

Burke's great disappointment at finding the depot party gone was made more bitter by the fact that he had given explicit instructions that they should await his return. And so the three men struggled on. Day after day Wills made entries in his diary. Two months after leaving Cooper's Creek, with no relief, his entries foretell the approaching end:

I am so weak as to be incapable of crawling out of the shelter...King is holding out well, but Burke finds himself weaker every day. They are preparing to go up the creek in search of natives who may be able to help us. I think this is our only chance. They will leave me some nardoo seeds and water, with which I must do the best I can until they return. They have both shown great hesitation and reluctance with regard to leaving me, but I have insisted that they go.

This is the last entry in the diary:

FRIDAY , 29TH JUNE, 1861. Clear, cold night, a light breeze from the east, day beautifully warm and pleasant. Mr Burke suffers greatly and is getting extremely weak. ...Nothing now but the greatest good luck can save any of us! and as for myself I may live four or five days if the weather continues warm. My pulse is at forty-eight, and very weak, and my legs and arms are nearly skin and bone...

With Wills dying in the shelter of the mia-mia, Burke and King made another attempt to contact natives in their search for food and help.

On the second day, after crawling for about two miles, Burke became too exhausted to go farther. They found some nardoo, and King shot a crow which enabled them to have a meal of sorts. But the leader of the great Across Australia expedition realised toward evening that he could not long survive. In a feeble voice he said to King, 'I hope you will remain with me here till I am quite dead; it is a comfort to know that someone is by; but when I am dying, it is my wish that you should place the pistol in my right hand, and that you leave me unburied as I lie.'

Burke died at eight o'clock on the following morning. King wandered down the creek until he fell in with a party of natives who treated him with every kindness. He had been living with them for a month when a search party arrived and rescued the sole survivor of the four men who had made the dash for the Gulf of Carpentaria and were the first to cross this continent from south to north.

God grant that whenever, soon or late,
Our course is run and our goal is reach'd,
We may meet our fate as steady and straight
As he whose bones in yon desert bleach'd;
No tears are needed—our cheeks are dry,
We have none to waste upon living woe;
Shall we sigh for one who has ceased to sigh,
Having gone, my friends, where we all must go?

THE SACRED NUGGET GOLDRUSH

Perhaps Australia's most sensational goldrush was that at Kanowna, in Western Australia. The year was 1898. The sleepy old town appeared to be in the doldrums, when suddenly wild rumours swept the district concerning the new young parish priest, Father Long, and the finding of a nugget of gold weighing, nearly a hundred pounds. The exciting news quickly circulated that some diggers had found the great nugget not far out of the town and had shown it to the priest who, because he was pledged to secrecy, was not allowed to divulge the names of the finders or the location where the nugget was unearthed. If anyone questioned the reliability of the rumours, their doubts must have been

dispelled when the newspapers at Kanowna and elsewhere published the report of the Sacred Nugget find as fact.

The news caused a sensation and put new life into Kanowna. As the weeks passed, public excitement increased and hundreds of diggers arrived by every boat from the eastern States. Nevertheless, no further gold finds were reported. The authorities pressed Father Long to disclose where the nugget had been found. After a time the distressed priest consented to make a public statement and reveal the locality of the mysterious find.

When the day and hour arrived several thousand diggers thronged the main street of Kanowna; everybody was ready to make a dash to the locality of the alleged find. There were buggies by the hundred, horses, camels, bicycles, all equipped with the necessary tools for pegging claims. Punctually, at the appointed time, Father Long appeared on the balcony of the building and faced the largest audience seen in the town. He looked pale and wan as he made his speech.

'I am here,' he began, 'as promised, to make a public statement regarding the finding of the so-called "Sacred Nugget". The newspapers, with their gross exaggeration, their distortion of facts, are entirely to blame for all these false reports, and the resultant turmoil. True, I was shown a nugget, but it was no immense slug of gold as I was reported to have stated. I cannot tell you the names of the finders, because I have not their permission. Nevertheless, I am able to tell you this. The nugget was found, according to what I was told, about a quarter of a mile on this side of the lake on the road to Kurnalpi...'

Nobody waited to hear further. Such a race was never before seen in Australia. Vehicles and pedestrians made a headlong rush along the narrow road leading to Kurnalpi. Everyone worked continuously that day securing claims and sinking holes, but not a patch of colour could be found. Soon it was realised that the rush had been a dud.

The truth about it all may never be known. The general opinion among the diggers was that it was a put-up job by the business people to attract money to the town. Also, that no blame could be attached to the young priest who, being of a trustful nature, was easily hood-winked. Feelings ran so high that some of the disappointed diggers talked of burning down Kanowna, or at least the business section.

Father Long was so upset by it all that it affected his health, and he died a few months later at the early age of twenty-seven.

THE FIRST LOTTERY

An economic disaster caused Australia's first lottery. New South Wales was hit by a great drought from 1838 that continued into the next decade and began to undermine the financial stability of the colony. Shop business dwindled, warehouses were unable to unload their stocks, and soon fortunes were being swept away as banks and companies crashed.

The Bank of Australia was among those that went insolvent and the liquidators in Sydney announced that they would raffle its assets—lands and businesses held as securities on dishonoured mortgages to the value of more than five million pounds. So was held the first public lottery in Australia, and it was a sensational event. Sydney went lottery crazy, and during the four days of the drawing in January 1849, crowds packing the City Theatre in Market Street were at fever pitch. Streets were all but deserted, but the lottery ticket sellers did a great business. Although lottery tickets were £4 each—a large sum in those days—there was scarcely a person who did not have at least a share, no matter how small, in a ticket.

Now that Sydney had succumbed to the lottery craze the Bank of Australia advertised that it would hold a further lottery to dispose of some remaining assets. Leading citizens began to wonder if private lotteries would solve their own financial difficulties. Always one to make the most of an opportunity, the astute lawyer and politician William Charles Wentworth decided to inaugurate a lottery for his own benefit. He realised that this would be a golden chance to dispose of some of the vast properties he held which because of the economic crash had dropped alarmingly in value on the current market.

Accordingly, it was announced by 'a group of public-spirited citizens' that they had 'persuaded' Mr Wentworth to dispose of his properties—'a large mass, such as it is believed no other single individual in the Colony is possessed of'—so that he might be able to devote his full time to the affairs of his country. (Much of Wentworth's properties had been acquired in lieu of payment from clients affected by the great depression.) It was planned to sell 12,000 tickets at £5 each with a prize for every ticket.

The 'prize for every ticket' was a sure-fire attraction and the general public was enthusiastic. Some of the more sober-minded citizens had misgivings and one newspaper ridiculed Wentworth's scheme, beginning its remarks with 'When a Patriot consents to be trotted out like a horse for so amazing a price, we think ourselves entitled to walk round him at our leisure. And we shall do so...' Among its many criticisms the newspaper editorial asserted that the price of a ticket could purchase more land than most were likely to win in the lottery.

Despite adverse criticism, applications for tickets poured in for the two lotteries being advertised side by side—William Charles Wentworth's and the Bank of Australia's. Then the Government began to have doubts about the outcome of such lotteries and so the Attorney-General called on Mr Wentworth and threatened to prosecute him; at the same time the liquidators of the Bank of Australia were also warned to discontinue their intentions of holding another lottery. Both lotteries were thereupon abandoned. Thirty-two years later when George Adams established his sweepstake in Sydney, it was a technical evasion of the law against lotteries, the prize awards being decided not entirely by the blind luck of the draw, but by a contingent sporting event.

In 1893 the Bank of Van Diemen's Land Ltd., Hobart, went into liquidation. Remembering how the Bank of Australia in Sydney had successfully disposed of most of its assets when in a similar plight, the Tasmanian bank decided to do likewise. The bank directors put the assets into a lottery—300,000 tickets at £1 each—the first prize being the bank building itself and the land on which it was built at Miller's Corner, Hobart. Second prize was a hotel, and all the other prizes consisted of bank properties in various places. Tickets were fully taken up. It is interesting to note that in 1955 a sweep was organised on the Melbourne Cup, offering as first prize Hadley's Orient Hotel at Hobart, which was officially valued by the Tasmanian State Treasury at £200,000.

THE WESTRALIA MINE RESCUE

This is the story of one of the most remarkable rescues in the history of Australian mining.

The Bonnievale district of the Kalgoorlie goldfields in Western Australia was not aptly named; it is neither a vale nor would it be described as bonny. At the time of this happening it was simply a dry and dusty patch of desert, though deep below its arid surface lay a rich reef of gold. The settlement consisted of some two hundred and fifty miners and their families, the men being employed in the Westralia Mine.

The rainfall of the district is so low that sometimes there is none for a whole year. But on the 20th March 1907 there was a sudden freak cloudburst which speedily flooded the plain. Torrential rain deafened the population as it battered onto their galvanised-iron homes and struck the hard-baked earth.

Within a few minutes the rushing waters were pouring down the Westralia Mine opening, gushing through the shaft into the passages of the lower levels. The miners needed no second telling to make for the surface. Terror-stricken men scrambled from the mine fighting against the flood-waters and debris pouring down the shaft. They ran along the dark passages splashing through water thigh-deep, and sometimes swimming—fighting their way to higher levels.

The roll was called as the soaked miners emerged, singly and in groups, to stand round the pithead, their rugged faces pale from their ordeal. When the mine manager checked the names of all present, he asked, 'Was anyone working with Varischetti? He's the one man missing.'

'He was on his own, working on a rock-drill on No. 10—the thousand-foot level,' said a miner. 'He wouldn't stand a chance, unless he got out immediately. The water's risen a hundred feet above that level. He'd be drowned like a rat in a trap.'

The manager tried not to sound pessimistic. 'There's always the thousand to one chance,' he commented. 'The engineer is studying the plan of the workings. Maybe he can offer some hope.'

When the manager joined the mine engineer, the latter pointed out to him on the plan a section of the mine marked No. 10 level. 'There's where Varischietti was working. The tunnel follows the reef with roughly a forty-five-degree incline from the ground horizon.' He paused and, turning to the mine manager, exclaimed, 'Say! There's a chance !'

'But how? What escape is there? The water must have filled the level. Why, it's filled the next level—No. 9—a hundred feet above it.'

'I know, but he's on a rise at the end of a tunnel. And the air can't escape. Air pressure will hold the water back!'

'Are you certain?'

'Well, in theory anyway. Look here! If you take a glass tumbler full of air, plunge its mouth downwards into a bucket of water, you imprison an air bubble. Something like that might have happened in No. 10 level, at the end of the tunnel.'

The manager looked dubious. 'Might have happened, as you say, but hardly likely. Do you think it's possible he could continue to exist in a large air bubble, imprisoned by water?'

'It's possible, though I admit not probable. But it's a logical theory.'

'Well, we'll put all the available pumping and bailing equipment to work. We'll have to lower the water from No. 9 level to No. 10. And that's going to take a few days, even working non-stop day and night.'

'Yes,' agreed the engineer, 'I should say at least ten days. But could a human being survive for ten days without food, in total darkness, imprisoned a thousand feet below ground?'

The manager shook his head. 'Surely not. The man's limited supply of air would become exhausted and heavily charged with carbonic acid gas. It would gradually suffocate him.'

'It looks hopeless,' admitted the engineer. 'Nevertheless, nobody knows for certain. Let's get things moving. Every minute is precious.'

A search party descended to No. 10 level and waded, knee-deep, to a point near the end that was thought to be about fifty feet vertically above the spot where Varischetti had been working. The light from the candles they carried threw grotesque shadows along the rocky roof and glistening walls of the tunnel. Only the faint throb of the distant pump and the lapping of water on stone disturbed the eerie underground silence. Here the party knocked heavily and rhythmically on the rock with a hammer, and then listened intently. Again and again they tried, but no reply came in answer to the signal.

'Poor devil!' remarked one of the miners. 'To think he lost his wife only a year ago. And those five kids depending on him!'

'We'll have to get together,' said another, 'and take care of the kids ourselves. At least we can look after 'em until things get fixed up somehow. Varischetti was always ready to help others. A better bloke you'd never meet.'

The men renewed their knocking, but again there was no response.

'It's no use. We had better give up.'

'Try just once more.'

Again they knocked, and listened, but this time the uncanny silence was broken by a very faint sound. They looked at each other, speechless, until they recognised that the sound was really a tapping one. Then they shouted with joy at the knowledge that Varischetti was alive.

Cheers and congratulations came from those round the mine head when they learnt the good news about the missing miner. Trapped in the waterlogged tunnel, he must have been exerting frantic efforts as he beat on the roof of his rocky prison trying to send signals to those who were doing their utmost to help him.

Now came the problem: how could he be rescued? The Inspector of Mines, summoned from Coolgardie, had arrived, but like everyone else could see no solution to the problem. A suggestion that a hole should be made down from one of the levels to where the miner was entombed was rejected because it was realised that, once the air was released from the chamber, water would rush in and drown the man. It would take ten days to pump out the water with the available pumps and bailing appliances, and the miner could never live so long without food.

On the evening of the third day the mine manager, depressed with worry, was in his home when the engineer came hurriedly to see him.

'You won't believe it!' he exclaimed. 'Young Billy has given us the solution for the rescue.'

'Billy? You mean your youngster?'

'Yes! A few minutes ago, at the dinner-table. I had just told the wife I had no appetite thinking of poor Varischetti. "If only," I said, "we could get some food to him to keep him alive till we could rescue him." Then up pipes young Billy and says, "Dad, why can't you send a man down the mine in one of those funny underwater dresses?"'

'A diver! Of course! "Out of the mouths of babes!" I'll send a telegram to Perth appealing for a diver. If one is available, he'll need to be sent on a special train. There won't be another one due for three days.'

Within twenty-four hours three deep-sea divers were at the mouth of the shaft. This was a job, however, far different to all their other experiences. The murky waters through which they made their way were illuminated by not the slightest ray of light; inside their heavy glass-mounted helmets they might as well have been blindfolded. There was the great danger, too, of the tunnels, weakened by the flood-waters, caving in and burying them for ever beneath tons of stone and silt.

One of the divers injured his leg and was unable to continue; a second man had to remain at the surface to attend the diving pump. It was left to diver Hughes to try and reach Varischetti. It was a long wait before a signal tug came from Hughes to let them know he was returning. Eventually he emerged from the water and stood swaying on his feet. Deft hands unbuckled his harness and unscrewed the helmet, as Hughes fell to the ground in a faint.

'Quick, give him a brandy,' said the second diver, as he massaged Hughes' limbs. 'No wonder he's collapsed: he's been down four times today, ten fathoms deep and a thousand feet underground. Not like diving in the sea, where the salt water buoys you up and you can see where you are. It's terrible down there.'

'He's opening his eyes. Feeling a bit better, mate?'

Hughes gave a wan smile. 'I'm right. The man's alive.'

The joyful news caused great excitement, but when diver Hughes asked for his helmet to be screwed on the men begged him to rest a while.

'No,' he said, 'I'm better already. I'd been trying to find the air-hose connected to the pneumatic rock-drill Varischetti had been using. I fumbled everywhere till I felt it, and then I followed it along the floor to the rise where he must have been drilling before he was caught. The going was tough, but I tugged at the hose as hard as I could. I was hoping it would rattle and make a noise to attract his attention. When there was no answer, I guessed he must be dead or unconscious. And then suddenly there came a pull on the line. I knew he was alive. But I was feeling so faint, I dared not go farther. I just about made the surface. I'll be right this time. Shove the helmet on.'

On this the fifth day the diver reached the terrified miner crouched on a rock shelving in pitch darkness. He gave the man food and pressed his hands in assurance that he would soon be rescued. During the next five days the diver made repeated trips to the entombed miner; it was too dangerous to put Varischetti in a diving suit. In the meantime water and slush were being pumped out day and night.

What were the entombed man's thoughts during the seemingly endless days and nights. This is what he had to say.

'I lost count of time. For hours I would crouch in the darkness, my mind blank. Then I would suddenly realise where I was. Fear gripped me at the thought of the terrible death I would suffer, and so I prayed for help and comfort. When the flood trapped me, I tried to swim through it, but the great pressure forced me back to the air pocket at the end of the tunnel. When the water stopped rising, I thought my prayers had been answered.

'My candle burnt out, and I was in pitch darkness without food. A long time after, when I heard the first tappings, I thought it was my imagination. Then I realised I would die of starvation before I could be reached. When the pipeline signal came, I did not understand. I saw it move and then I pulled it. I thought I must be slowly going mad. And when the diver came, it was the most terrible moment of all. I heard splashing and something heavy move in the water. There was only one match left; I struck it with trembling hands. What I saw made me gasp in terror. A hideous head of a monster was coming out of the water. As the match went out, I made the sign of the cross ....'

On the tenth day of his terrible ordeal Varischetti was carried out on the shoulders of diver Hughes. He had collapsed and was seriously ill; after long medical treatment and rest, however, he was able to resume his place as breadwinner for his five children. The heroic Hughes also needed hospital treatment for some time. Today his name is inscribed on the honour roll of mining heroes.

THE MAGPIE PROFESSOR
In the chronicles of early Melbourne a writer of that period records that a curious magpie belonged to the keeper of the Melbourne Pound for strayed cattle. Such were the gifts natural and acquired of this extraordinary bird that he was known as the Professor.

The magpie had received a limited education, not taught at Sunday school. His language was very bad, and some of his expressions, though choice, were extremely inelegant. He picked up low talk from the ex-convict bullock-drivers and stockmen with whom he consorted. The Professor was always flying into public houses and calling for a pot of beer. Often, when he had indulged in too much liquid refreshment, he would sink into the besotted condition that would justify a policeman in locking him up, not only as a drunken and disorderly character but for using bad language.

'One Sunday afternoon the Professor, through a desire to shake off the effects of a heavy spree, started from the Pound for a stroll up the Yarra. Governor Lonsdale resided in the comfortable Government House at the western end of Yarra Park. The inmates, with the exception of the lady of the mansion and a maid-servant, had gone to church. The Governor's lady was reading her Bible aloud in her private sitting-room when the Professor hopped in noiselessly. The bird stationed himself in a corner and for some time was an unseen and attentive listener.

'Suddenly the good lady was thunderstruck by hearing within a few feet of where she sat a cracked, screaming voice bidding her to be off at once to an unmentionable region. Turning round in extreme alarm she saw that the intruder was a bird—certainly not a bird of

Paradise. While hesitating as to summoning assistance to eject the unholy visitor the disturber solved the uncertainty for her by ejaculating a stunning oath or two and making his exit through the open window.

'One of the Professor's many accomplishments was an art he had acquired through listening at the frequently held Pound sales. He would often make bids at auction sales, to the confusion of buyers and vendors and the joy of the crowds attending the auction sales.'

But the Professor came to a sad end. This strange bird, more inebriated than usual, staggered from a hotel, tumbled into the Yarra River and was drowned.

SHOW BUSINESS

Sydney was excited in the late 1890s over a report that a marble man, whose estimated age was one million years, had been discovered near Bathurst, New South Wales. He was stated to have been found in a limestone cave. The finder of the marble man, an Italian, it was announced, had sold it to a Scotsman, who had bought it out of curiosity. But, because of the intense interest the figure was causing, the new owner decided to make money with it as a sideshow exhibit. So the petrified gentleman was placed in a large box, brought to Sydney, and put on show: admission one shilling, children half-price (if accompanied by parents or guardian).

However, there were sceptics who hinted that the marble man was a fraud, merely carved by someone skilled in monumental work. A local scientist subjected the dubious ancestor of the aborigine to close scrutiny and then declared in the *Sydney Morning Herald* that he was indeed a fake. The proprietor indignantly refused to accept 'expert' opinion. After all, the marble man was coining money. So an eminent doctor, a very well-known Macquarie Street practitioner, was called in. The doctor, after sawing off a finger, gave a statement to the Press that he would stake his professional reputation on the absolute genuineness of the find. He said that, under a microscope, he had detected bone and tissue structure—human flesh petrified. The marble man, whoever he was, had come to Australia a million years before the white man, perhaps even before the coming of the black man.

70

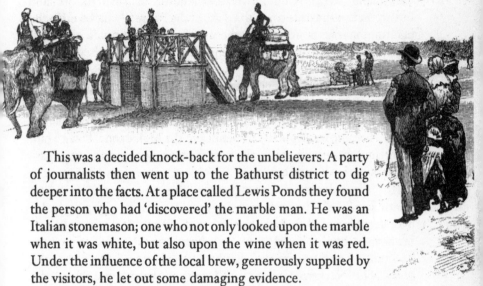

This was a decided knock-back for the unbelievers. A party of journalists then went up to the Bathurst district to dig deeper into the facts. At a place called Lewis Ponds they found the person who had 'discovered' the marble man. He was an Italian stonemason; one who not only looked upon the marble when it was white, but also upon the wine when it was red. Under the influence of the local brew, generously supplied by the visitors, he let out some damaging evidence.

The reporters then nosed their way into a cave and, with the aid of a lantern, found the place where the figure had made his bed for a million years, more or less. At least, the marble block out of which the stonemason had carved the effigy must have been a million years old. And so the show was ended.

Lots of people, including the distinguished doctor, had to unsay a great deal of foolish things they had been quoting and writing about Darwin, the origin of the species, and such like. Worse still, the public began to demand back its admission money, whereupon the proprietor of the show—the Scotsman—appeared to be as furious as anyone about the deception. He asserted that he had sincerely believed the 'find' to be genuine when he bought it from the Italian, and had made an agreement with the latter that he would give him half the profits from exhibiting it. In view of the exposure of the fake he refused to give the Italian a penny; instead, he donated the stonemason's fifty per cent to a Sydney hospital.

In the National Gallery of Victoria in Melbourne can be seen a magnificent bushfire painting by Sir John Longstaff entitled

'Gippsland'. Impressive as it is in all its majestic realism of the doomed forest, there was a time when the glare of the fire really flickered in the painting, smoke poured from the picture, and hundreds of people actually heard and smelt the burning of the forest whilst they gazed in awe at this wonderful painting!

This is how it all happened. A well-known showman and theatrical identity, H. D. Annear, was so impressed with the realism of Longstaff's painting of the tragic Gippsland bushfire of 1898 that he decided to make a fortune for the artist. He engaged the Melbourne Town Hall, hung the picture with a rail well out in front, and put in a system of gas-burners with an attachment in which gum-leaves and twigs were burnt. It was all cleverly concealed, and the publicity stunt caused a minor sensation. However, one day an elderly short-sighted gentleman determined to find out how it was all done. He got too close to the heaters, had his beard burnt, and almost caused a panic in the hall. As a result Longstaff decided that he had had enough and closed the show. The National Gallery of Victoria afterwards purchased the painting from him—needless to say, without the effects.

Harry Rickards, the famous owner-entrepreneur of the Tivoli Theatres, although a shrewd business man and a powerful influence in show business, was a slave to superstition. His circuit was Australia-wide, and in every capital city his theatres showed the best that Australia could produce, and the best that high salaries could tempt from the leading theatres of the world. Horseshoes adorned his office; he refused to do business on Fridays; he recoiled from the number thirteen and was ever watchful not to walk under any of the ladders backstage.

Probably the most remarkable outburst in the history of the Tivoli Theatre, Sydney, occurred when an artist brought out from England on a very large salary swept onto the stage with regal dignity, clad from head to foot in green. And to make matters worse the orchestra struck up the famous tune of Tosti's 'Good-bye', considered to be the theatre's most unlucky song. For a second Rickards was thunderstruck, but only for a second. Then, rising wrathfully in his box, he shouted, 'Out of my theatre! Out! Out!'

This sensational debut ruined the artist's Australian season. Rickards never saw her again, but he certainly heard from her lawyer. It cost him a small fortune, but he preferred the loss to having a hoodoo over his theatre.

Although the legitimate theatre has passed through many vicissitudes in Australia, as elsewhere, nevertheless there have always been enthusiasts to keep it alive: individuals who dreamed and worked and were filled with a burning zeal that far exceeded their sadly limited technical and artistic ability. And zeal is no mean thing. One of the most extraordinary phenomena in theatre history was the number of theatrical performances given by convicts in the early days.

The birth of Australian theatre was accompanied by a chorus of clanking leg-irons. With all the miseries of remoteness and starvation in the penal settlement of New South Wales, convicts found time and enthusiasm just a little more than a year after the arrival of the First Fleet in 1788 to give Australia its first taste of theatrical fare. This was an amateur production of *The Recruiting Officer*, a lusty Restoration play which would need some blue-pencilling today in order to get past the censor. Thus in a mud and daub building, with only a rough stage and with backless benches for the motley audience, was the theatre born in Australia.

Eleven convicts comprised the cast for *The Recruiting Officer*. Coloured paper decorated the mud hut, while farthing dips lit the customers to their seats, and a few oil lamps were used for footlights. Since money was so very scarce, admittance was in kind: rum, tobacco, spirits, wheat and such like to the value of £20 were taken at the door. It was a capacity audience, and the sixty people present included Governor Phillip and his officers.

Seven years later Robert Sidaway, a former convict who had become the settlement's first baker, built the Botany Bay Theatre in what is now Bligh Street, Sydney. The theatre was built mainly of saplings, and it held about one hundred and twenty people. Admission ranged from one shilling in the gallery to five shillings for boxes. If the theatregoer was short of ready cash (as indeed most were), he could give the equivalent in food or the inevitable liquor. Although a commercial success, the Botany Bay Theatre lasted but two years. Many of the ex-convicts still retained their old itch, and it was their wont to go to the playhouse, observe who was in the audience, and then depart to rob their homes at leisure. Things came to such a pass that Governor John Hunter had the playhouse demolished.

Undeterred by this disaster, Sidaway presented plays elsewhere. These included musical entertainment, abridged versions of Shakespeare, and a revival of *The Recruiting Officer*. A member of Sidaway's company was George Hughes, the colony's first printer. During this period amateur performances were sometimes held in large rooms in private homes.

About the year 1800 there appeared a phenomenon in the shape of 'theatres' on wheels. These travelling shows, in which illicit performances were given, were run by pedlars and low characters. In 1826 a strange theatre was the debtors' room of the Sydney jail, where the prisoners staged typical melodramas of those times. The respectable, but curious public were allowed to see these plays through the window grates.

The name Barnett Levey is associated with the real beginnings of commercial theatre in Australia. He built a playhouse in Sydney in close proximity to his Royal Hotel in George Street. He probably reasoned that a mellowed audience would be more likely to overlook the shortcomings, which must have been numerous judging by Press reports.

But no play reviews were as bad as those to be found in the journal called *Tigg's Monthly*. This was the sensation of theatrical life in the Sydney of the 1830s. The pretentious publication was so hostile to the theatre that it not only panned almost every show that was produced, but attempted to dictate the morals of the artists. Reviewing a new play at Barnett Levey's playhouse, *Tigg's Monthly* said:

'The premiere of *The Miller's Daughter* was an utter fiasco. It was rather run through than acted. The burning of the mill failed; pistols were fired at the wrong moment; and the curtain fell to hide the confusion of those behind it.

'But worse was to follow. The leading lady, Maria Taylor, came forward to lead the company in the singing of the national anthem. But whether it was from any remains of her pristine modesty, or that she had imbibed too freely of the wine bottle, we were unable to decide which of the two rendered her utterly unable to make even a tolerable attempt at singing.

'Readers will recall that it was this same lady who, on her last visit to this town, scandalised Sydney by her affair with a local merchant, John Thomas Nilson. As a result, he was the subject of a popular jingle entitled "The Family Man", the last four lines of which we quote:

He would have married her long ago
(He's of the marrying kidney),
But when one has a wife at home,
One can't have one in Sydney.

Hobart and Launceston started to develop theatrical history at the same time as Sydney. It is a fact that at one period in the first quarter of the nineteenth century Tasmania was leading the rest of Australia in all theatrical matters, amateur and professional. Indeed, Tasmania supplied Sydney, Melbourne, and Adelaide with managers, actors, and plays that had been tried out first in Launceston or Hobart.

The early Australian theatres continued a tradition of versatility. It was the usual custom for the bill of fare on any programme to be well mixed. Thus, patrons would be treated to perhaps drama, song and dance, comedy, and recitations, all on the one programme.

The main factor that transformed the Australian theatre from a struggling, semi-amateur affair into a fully fledged and prosperous profession was the finding of gold and the consequent extraordinary increase in population and wealth. Many English artists came to this country, some of whom were first-raters. One favourite actress was Jenny Blair, a pretty little dramatic artist who, on one occasion while travelling by coach from Sydney to Bathurst, was waylaid by a masked bushranger. However, when the latter discovered the identity of his victim, he handed back her possessions with profuse apologies.

Some days later, while Jenny Blair was appearing in Bathurst, there came to the hotel where she was staying a young man seeking her autograph. He mentioned that he had not missed one night of her performances and intended to frame her autograph. Miss Blair acquiesced, but when her visitor left she wondered why his voice seemed familiar. Then she recalled the masked man that held up her coach. She immediately informed the police station, and the bushranger was caught.

At his trial Jenny Blair was the chief Crown witness. But when her eyes met those of the reproachful prisoner she burst into tears, saying, 'I should never have informed on him! Please, your Honour, give him a chance! He's only a boy—barely out of his teens. I know he has committed a crime, but by nature he is gracious and kind-hearted. I beg of you to show him mercy!'

Despite her pleadings the twenty-year-old bushranger was condemned to death and hanged.

Whatever the quality by modern standards, Australian theatre history has rare colour and glamour. In the 1890s such men as George Farrell, Dan Barry, Alfred Dampier, and William Anderson wrote Australian plays that were a roaring success. Their plays were dotted with impressive spectacles: corroborees, holding up a gold escort, bushfires and real horse-races. One play, a tale of the Melbourne Cup, had twenty thoroughbred horses racing. The back of the stage had been removed and a huge backcloth hung on the buildings on the opposite side of the street. Thus, the audience witnessed the spectacle of the horses racing along the street outside the theatre.

Great names sprinkled the latter half of the nineteenth century: Nellie Stewart, Maggie Moore, George Coppin, Edwin Booth, Boucicault, and the immortal queen of tragedy, Sarah Bernhardt. At Bernhardt's premiere in Melbourne the gay young bloods of the town unyoked the horses from her carriage and pulled it to her hotel, to the cheering of the crowds. The Divine Sarah disliked the Australian summer, and when playing in Melbourne she would often call her brougham between acts and drive to St Kilda for the sea breeze, keeping the audience awaiting her pleasure.

ART SURPRISES

In Melbourne is an intriguing picture of that city in its infancy, painted by the architect, Samuel, who designed Melbourne's St Francis'

Church in Elizabeth Street, and also the first St Patrick's Church. A panorama of Melbourne, this picture was lost for many years, but was eventually found locked up in a government safe. In order to paint it, Samuel got into a large beer barrel and, removing a stave, sketched what he saw through the opening. The stave was replaced and the next stave removed, and so on until the panorama was completed.

An unusual painting in the National Gallery of Victoria in Melbourne is entitled 'Don Quixote'. Seated on his charger, Don Quixote is seen directing his armies (a flock of sheep) in the valley below. Don's faithful servant is descending the hill on a donkey. Only on close inspection does one discover that in the sky, cunningly painted to resemble clouds, is a regiment of handsome white horses.

One of the best-known paintings in the Art Gallery of New South Wales in Sydney is George Lambert's 'Across the Blacksoil Plains'. The artist has caught the very spirit of that remarkable area around Pilliga known as the Blacksoil Plains, in which he depicts a fine team of horses hauling a wagon loaded with wool. When it was first exhibited, critics went into ecstasies over the masterpiece, but the first bushman to see the picture was shocked at the artist's mistake. Not one horse in the team has a belly-band. To be sure, horses are sometimes used without them, but never in a team hauling such a big load across the Blacksoil Plains.

Mistakes by artists bring to mind the many inaccuracies to be found on Australian stamps. There was quite a rumpus caused by the 1947 stamp commemorating the 150th anniversary of Newcastle. It had a portrait of the wrong man as the discoverer of Newcastle! A later five-shillings stamp showed the wrong coat-of-arms for South Australia.

The 1938 stamp issued during the sesquicentenary of Australia's foundation features a portrait of Governor Phillip in full naval uniform and wearing epaulets. However, epaulets were not worn by naval men at the time of Phillip's arrival in this country. Other uniform errors can be seen in the 1940 stamps commemorating Australia's participation in World War II. The stamps carry a common motif of an airman, sailor, soldier, and nurse. But the airman wears on his breast only half a wing instead of the full spread, and the penny stamp shows the soldier carrying a rifle with a broken butt.

In 1927 commemorative stamps were issued to mark the opening of the Federal Parliament House at Canberra. The stamp shows the flag flying from the top of the Parliament building at half mast. Maybe the designer had a sense of humour.

The Victorian centenary stamp of 1934 is a fine study of the city of Melbourne as seen from across the Yarra. An Aborigine, a member of the extinct Yarra Yarra tribe, is included in the scene. What's wrong? Well, 1934 was the centenary of the first settlement in Victoria, but that was at Portland Bay. Melbourne was not founded until 1835.

The lyrebird featured on the one-shilling stamp first issued in 1932 is inaccurate. The bird's body is shown facing the left, and the tail feathers to the front—a physical impossibility.

The 1934 stamp specially issued to celebrate the centenary of the death of Captain John Macarthur, a founder of Australia's wool industry, depicts a champion merino ram. If the picture is closely examined, you will see ingeniously camouflaged on the wool of the rump of the animal the head of a man. It resembles Macarthur, but is probably unintentional.

Stamp collectors rate as their best prizes those stamps in which the designers make mistakes. Even tiny and apparently insignificant errors make these stamps more valuable. In recent years an Australian collector came across a 2d stamp bearing the portrait of King George VI which showed a wide line reaching from the King's mouth to the bottom of the stamp. The printing flaw resembles a large cigar. The defect increased the stamp's value considerably.

In 1913 a kangaroo appeared on Commonwealth stamps, poised in the centre of a map of Australia. So abused was the die of this design that in some stamps the marsupial appeared with a broken tail, a cut throat, and occasionally was found to have two tails.

The 1931 stamp commemorating the many world flights of Sir Charles Kingsford Smith depicts the *Southern Cross* flying above the two hemispheres. A technical error in a number of copies was caused by an inkspot. It looks like a bomb dropping from the plane and being directed at Australia.

A Poor Simple Fool

Beachcombing is almost a profession in Broome, on the north-west coast of Western Australia. Certainly its members are not exactly dead-beats. If you want to gather shell, or the flotsam and jetsam found on the wide, white sweep of Broome's tidewashed beaches, you must obtain a beachcomber's licence.

Perhaps the richest treasure trove ever found by a beachcomber in this area was that of the packet of diamonds valued at more than £20,000 picked up by John Palmer. The gems were found at Carnot Bay, north of Broome, and their discovery led to a sensational story.

When on 18th February, 1942, Port Darwin was bomb-blitzed, a new seaplane base was hastily improvised a Broome in an attempt to maintain the air services from Australia to Java. It was only a matter of days, however, before the Japanese invasion of Java was begun and soon the Dutch defences collapsed.

On 3rd March Captain Ivan Smirnoff, in command of a Dutch airliner, made an emergency flight from the Bandung airport in Java to Broome. He had a crew of three, and eight passengers: six Dutchmen and one woman with a baby. It was an escape of refugees, fleeing at the last moment from the fast approaching Japanese. Just before the take-off a bank messenger arrived with a sealed package for Captain Smirnoff. It was from the Bank of Java and was addressed to the Commonwealth Bank of Australia. The package was placed in the cockpit, and the plane set off on its course to Broome, about ten hours' flying time, across water all the way. When the Australian coast was sighted, those aboard the plane were cheered that everything had gone so smoothly, but suddenly three Japanese Zero fighters dive-bombed them. They had reached the Australian coast at the time of a Japanese air raid on Broome.

The enemy sent a hail of bullets into the airliner, and Captain Smirnoff was shot through both arms and in the thigh. The port engine burst into flames, but he managed to keep the plane under control and make a landing on the beach at the water's edge. The woman passenger and her baby were both dead. So also was the mechanic. The others, all bleeding from wounds, lay on that beach for five days before help came to them. It was a miracle that they survived.

They owed their lives to a wild Aborigine. Nobody knew that the plane had been shot down at Carnot Bay except the Japanese responsible and this lone nomadic native. He walked forty-five miles to the nearest abode of white men, the Beagle Bay Mission, to tell what he had seen. The Reverend Brother Richards immediately set out with a rescue party, taking two mule carts, provisions and medical supplies. It took fifteen hours non-stop to reach the scene of the tragedy.

It was not until some three weeks later that an official party visited the wreck. Captain Smirnoff had told them of the sealed package in the cockpit of the plane, but they found no package, only a piece of string with two seals attached. In the meantime the Commonwealth Bank had been advised by the Bank of Java of the packet of diamonds valued at £20,500 that had been dispatched on the ill-fated plane.

About two months later a man walked into the recruiting office at Broome to enlist in the Australian Army. He gave his name, John Palmer, single, and age forty-seven. Asked his occupation, he said, 'Oh, a bit of everything. I own a lugger, but it's no use to me.' Then, with a smile, he added, 'Put me down as a beachcomber.'

John Palmer passed the medical test and was sworn in as a member of the AIF. He then walked over to the officer and casually handed him a package, one end of which he had opened to show the contents. The officer glanced at it with indifference and asked, 'What are these stones? They look like diamonds.'

The officer was startled at the new recruit's reply, 'Oh, they're the dinkum stuff all right. There are over four and a half thousand cut diamond in that package. I know, because I counted them! They're worth a ruddy fortune.'

Scarcely able to believe his ears, the officer asked John Palmer where he got them, and why was he handing them into the Army?

'Well,' said Palmer, 'I found that packet of diamonds a few miles up north, on the beach at Carnot Bay. Some of the stones had fallen out of the parcel into the sand. I don't know how many of 'em were lost, but I don't think too many. Anyway,' he added as an afterthought, 'I guess the Army or the police are the ones to take charge of 'em.'

Private Palmer was taken to the Commanding Officer for further questioning, and was later placed under arrest. The diamonds, of course, were the contents of the package on the tragic flight. After Palmer's arrest two other men at Broome were found to have some diamonds for which they could not give a satisfactory explanation. These two men were also arrested and put on trial with Palmer.

It was alleged by the prosecution that Beachcomber Palmer sailed into Carnot Bay in his lugger, about ten days after the crash; that he entered the derelict plane and slept in it for one night; that he stole the packet of diamonds, then sailed away. At Broome he gave or sold a few of the diamonds to the other two men on trial.

Defending counsel for Palmer said that he was amazed that his client should be prosecuted at all. He would have thought him entitled to a reward as a tribute to his honesty. He stressed the fact that all the gems had been recovered. It would have been an easy matter, in the general confusion of the times, for Palmer to get away in his lugger with the portable fortune he had found. Instead, he enlisted in the Army when at his age, forty-seven, he was not liable for conscription. Furthermore, after enlisting, he voluntarily handed over the fortune of diamonds to the authorities.

'Gentlemen of the jury,' said defending counsel, 'my client Private John Palmer, to put it plainly, is a poor simple fool.' All three accused were found not guilty.

PEOPLE OF THE PAST

The Curate of Hoole; Pioneers; Queen of the Hunter Valley;
The King of New Zealand; Sir John Robertson; Rose de Freycinet;
The Prince of Australia; The Flying Pieman; Cole of the Book Arcade;
The Autograph King; Women on the Map; The Wild White Man;
White Women with Natives; King Boongarie.

THE CURATE OF HOOLE

Why did Captain Cook come to Australia? Most people consider that it began when William Dampier, the English buccaneer, returned from his voyages and roused the interest of London with reports of what he had seen on the western side of this strange southern land. The fact remains, however, that it was a young parson addicted to star-gazing who set in motion the sequence of events that led Cook to these shores.

On the morning of 24th November, 1639, the Reverend Jeremiah Horrocks, twenty-two-year-old curate of the sleepy little village of Hoole, in Lancashire, woke up with an excited mind. It was a Sunday, and, though all his thoughts were of heavenly matters, they were not exclusively spiritual. At Cambridge, Horrocks had graduated as a brilliant mathematician, and after entering the Church he had given every spare moment to his hobby of astronomy.

His telescope, his most precious possession, had cost him half a crown, a sizeable sum in those days for a married man on a salary of fifteen shillings a week. No wonder Jeremiah was excited. It was his belief that on this day the planet Venus would pass between the earth and the sun. With the aid of his telescope and a screen he had set up in his darkened sitting room, he hoped to see, if conditions were favourable, the shadow of Venus creeping across the sunlit circle. Since the beginning of the world such an event in space had never been scientifically observed. Months of work had gone into making Jeremiah's intricate calculations and preparations for this day of days.

Although the Polish astronomer Copernicus had proved a century before that the earth and planets go round the sun, there were few people who believed his strange theory; indeed, few people could even understand what that sixteenth-century Einstein was talking about. But Jeremiah Horrocks knew that the theory was right. Moreover, with his little half-a-crown telescope he was able to see hitherto unknown heavenly wonders like the mountains on the moon, spots on the sun, the satellites of Jupiter, and the ring of Saturn.

A chance discovery by a Dutchman in 1608 had made it possible the following year for the Italian astronomer Galileo to put glasses together and so construct a telescope. Now, thirty years later, the young English curate was to reach another milestone in astronomical history.

Though it was a winter's day, Jeremiah saw with delight that the sun was shining. Sunlight shone into the telescope and made a bright circle on the screen in the darkened room. He longed to watch that bright circle all day, but this was the sabbath and his clerical duties would claim him until 3.15 in the afternoon.

When he hurried back from church to his humble cottage, he was overjoyed to see that the sun was still shining. Quickly entering the dim sitting-room, he looked at the screen. There crawling over the sunlit circle was a black spot! Jeremiah uttered a prayer of thanksgiving. 'O, Lord God, how Thy marvels exalt Thee!' For just on half an hour, until the sun set, he watched the moving figure. It was the crowning achievement of his short life.

Jeremiah Horrocks died in the following year, aged twenty-three.

But his work lived on. His writings revealed that he was a very great astronomer, and from his data it was possible to predict future transits of Venus. Of course, sometimes a century or more might elapse before conditions would be right to observe the transit, and many astronomers would never have the opportunity to make observations.

Thus, when in 1716 the sixty-year-old astronomer Edmond Halley, of comet fame, foresaw that a transit of Venus would take place forty-five years hence, and again in 1769, he left a memorial to British astronomers entreating them not to neglect these occasions. As a result, in 1760 the Royal Society, assisted by the British Government, organised expeditions to St Helena and Sumatra to make the observations.

Unfortunately the sky was clouded at St Helena on the great day; and the Sumatra ship was attacked by the French and never reached the East Indies. In consequence, the Royal Society was particularly anxious that the transit of 1769 should be observed with every care. They wrote to their patron, George III, praising His Majesty's 'remarkable love of science' and begging his help. George III was interested in science, but the £4,000 requested by the society for the expedition was a large sum. Fortunately the British Government was beginning to take an interest in the South Pacific at the time and the money was found.

There was another hitch, however. A captain was needed who must not only be a first-rate seaman and an officer of the King's Navy but also a first-rate astronomer. Luckily, a man with those specialised qualifications could be found. He was James Cook, then aged thirty-nine. He was skilled in seamanship and map making, a good mathematician and, like Jeremiah Horrocks, took a keen interest in astronomy. Captain Cook won the full approval of the councillors of the Royal Society.

So the party of scientific men sailed for Tahiti, and in the clear bright region of the tropic sky witnessed the heavenly phenomenon that had been studied for the first time more than a century previously by the young curate of Hoole. When Venus had been observed, the good ship *Endeavour* went roaming and came to the haven of Botany Bay.

PIONEERS

To the pioneer women in every State Australia owes deep respect for the foundations they laid for the life of this country. They were the backbone of the beginnings of Australia.

The first white woman to arrive in Victoria was Mrs Stephen Henty. She came as a bride in 1836, and was only nineteen at the time. One can imagine the excitement her arrival must have caused. Later she was to befriend Mrs Alexander Laurie, the remarkable pioneer woman who became editor of the *Portland Herald*. Mrs Laurie has left on record many of her impressions and accounts of the first settlement in Victoria.

'We landed by moonlight on a Sunday night, and I was carried on shore through the surf by a sailor. But what an out-of-the-world place it was!

'The people were very kind to me, especially Mrs Henty. She told me how much she had felt the want of a woman's company when she arrived there as the first white woman. She had engaged a housekeeper to travel with her but on the day of sailing the woman refused to go, someone having told her she would be eaten by cannibals.'

Mrs Laurie describes her new home in Portland thus:

'Our house was barely a shelter from sun and rain. The wind whistled through the place while the rain came down the chimney in torrents and put out the fire. Stout, unbleached calico was tacked to the walls, shingles were laid loosely on the ground and covered with a thick carpet. A shallow case with a shelf put in and covered with some black linen served to hold books. Draped boxes were used for side-tables, and a few flowers and foliage soon made it more habitable. Nevertheless, in spite of a roaring fire the cold south-west wind could not be kept out.

'That winter an umbrella protected my bed when the rain came from a certain quarter. At other times the outlook would have suited an astronomer—there was ample opportunity for studying the stars through the open parts ....'

In those days not only was there a new country to face, there was also the fear of the wild Aborigines. Mrs Laurie gives these instances.

'On one occasion a party of warlike natives approached a homestead on the outskirts of Portland. The men were all away at the time, so when the women saw the natives coming they dressed up in the men's clothes and went outside and stamped about near the house! The natives took fright and cleared off, thinking that the men were at home.

'I remember a woman who lived a little distance away and who was sometimes obliged to be alone all day while her husband was out with the stock. One day when she was bathing her baby, who was only two weeks old, natives walked one by one into her little home until they had filled it. She was terrified, but discovered that all they wanted was to see the white baby.'

Babies were reared under difficulties in the bush. It was a common sight to see a mother milking cows and at the same time rocking a cradle with one foot. Cradles were masterpieces of makeshift. Sometimes they consisted of a sheet of stringybark, which was allowed to curl so that it would rock easily. The ends were closed with flat sheets of bark. Another type of bush cradle was simply a section of a hollow log split open. A bush pram often consisted of a packing-case mounted on wooden wheels cut from a solid rock. Such a heavy and strong vehicle could withstand the rugged country in which it was used. Certainly, despite such rough rearing, bush babies grew into sturdy and hardy children.

In the 1880s a teamster left his wife and children on his selection in the New South Wales district of Narrabri for a two months' season of wool-carrying in Queensland. He left enough provisions to last his family until he came back, but floods prevented his return and soon the family was starving. The mother decided to get her three children, one a three-month-old baby, to the township of Narrabri. She hoped the two older children, one five, the other three, could walk while she carried the baby. But a quarter of a mile from her home the children were both tired of walking in the heavy black soil. So she carried them one by one: left the baby with the oldest child, took the second as far as she could without losing sight of the others, then put it down; returned for the baby, and made a third trip for the oldest child. When the mother and children were picked up, just out of Narrabri, the mother was unconscious; she did not know how many days and nights the eleven-mile trip had taken. In all, she had walked sixty-six miles carrying children thirty-three miles of the way. Mother and children were cared for in the township, and all recovered.

In the little Richmond River town of Coraki, in New South Wales, diaries of some of the early pioneers have been carefully preserved. Reading these diaries, one is struck by the fact that a great problem in those days was getting married. The nearest clergyman was a hundred miles away at Grafton, and it was an impossible journey to take. A cedar-getter and his girl, having no means of getting there, married themselves by throwing a stone into the river and vowing to be true to each other 'till the stone floated'.

Another couple got tired after months of waiting and, according to the woman's diary, she proposed this solution: 'We can't go round the world looking for a clergyman. Let us begin together and get married when one turns up.' The man agreed and years later when a clergyman did arrive at the outlandish village he performed not only the marriage ceremony, but the baptism of their seven youngsters.

'The greatest of women pioneers in the history of Australia.' Thus has been described the philanthropist Caroline Chisholm. The remarkable English-born Mrs Chisholm did tremendous charitable work in

CAROLINE CHISOLM

caring for women immigrants who found themselves stranded and penniless on arrival in Sydney. She made arrangements to place girls in situations in country areas, and in order to see them safely settled accompanied parties far afield. It was her determined efforts, also, that led to more humane treatment of immigrants on the long voyage to Australia, and she persuaded the British Government to grant free passages for the wives and families of convicts sent out at earlier dates.

Caroline Chisholm insisted that ships were not to be overcrowded, that they were to have an adequate supply of good food, well-ventilated sleeping accommodation and proper sanitary arrangements. The powerful shipowners opposed all this and bitterly attacked the innovator; nevertheless, Mrs Chisholm won her battle. In the first six years of her zeal for the poor and needy she cared for more than eleven thousand people, relieving much distress and transforming paupers into happy, industrious workers. Robert Lowe said of her work: 'It was the most original ever devised or undertaken by man or woman, and the object, the labour and the method were beyond all praise.' Michelet, the French historian, wrote of her: 'The fifth part of the world, Australia, has up to now but one saint, one legend. This saint is an Englishwoman . . . .' London *Punch* said she was 'a second Moses, in bonnet and shawl', and Florence Nightingale declared that she was proud to be Mrs Chisholm's 'friend and pupil'.

Caroline Chisholm came to Australia with her husband, Captain Chisholm, in 1838 and lived in Hobart, Adelaide, and Sydney, before taking up residence at Windsor. She paid a visit to England in 1846, but returned to Australia eight years later. She believed that a sound system of emigration was the best means of coping with the problem of overpopulation in Great Britain. To promote a desire for people of the 'old country' to make their homes in Australia, she interviewed many settlers to find out to what extent they had benefited in this new land, and to publicise the information. And so was published *Voluntary Information from the People of New South Wales*. Here is one of the many family case histories she obtained. In a footnote to this interview Caroline Chisholm described Joseph Smith as follows: 'He was an old man, with a large-featured, handsome, military sort of face, of a red-brown complexion, shaved clean. His dress consisted of a red flannel shirt, with a black bandanna, tied sailor-fashion, exposing his strong neck, and a pair of fustian trousers. Out of compliment to me he once put on a blue coat with gilt buttons, but, being evidently uncomfortable, consented to take it off again.'

Macdonald's River,
County of Hunter,
3rd October, 1845

I arrived in the colony fifty-six years ago; it was Governor Phillip's time, and I was fourteen years old; there were only eight houses in the colony then. I know that myself and eighteen others laid in a hollow tree for seventeen weeks, and cooked out of a kettle with a wooden bottom: we used to stick it in a hole in the ground, and make a fire round it. I was seven years in bondage, and then started working for a living wherever I could get it.

There was plenty of hardship then: I have often taken grass, pounded it, and made soup from a native dog. I would eat anything then. For seventeen weeks I had only five ounces of flour a day. We never got a full ration except when a ship was in harbour. The motto was 'Kill them, or work them, their provision will be in store.' Many a time have I been yoked like a bullock with twenty or thirty others to drag along timber. About eight hundred died in six months at a place called Toongabbie, or Constitution Hill.

I knew a man so weak, he was thrown into the grave, when he said, 'Don't cover me up; I'm not dead; for God's sake don't cover me up!' The overseer answered, 'Damn your eyes, you'll die tonight, and we shall have the trouble to come back again!' The man recovered; his name is James Glasshouse, and he is now alive at Richmond.

They used to have a large hole for the dead; once a day men were sent down to collect the corpses of prisoners, and throw them in without any ceremony or service. The native dogs used to come down at night and fight and howl in packs, gnawing the poor dead bodies.

The governor would order the lash at the rate of five hundred, six hundred or eight hundred; and if the men could have stood it they would have had more. I knew a man hung there and then for stealing a few biscuits, and another for stealing a frock. A man was condemned—no time—take him to the tree and hang him. The overseers were allowed to flog the men in the fields. Often have men been taken from the gang, given fifty, and sent back to work.

Any man would have committed murder for a month's provisions: I would have committed three murders for a week's provisions! I was chained seven weeks on my back for being out getting greens, wild herbs. The Rev Samuel Marsden used to come it tightly to force some confession. Men were obliged to tell lies to prevent their bowels from being cut out by the lash. The laws were bad then. If an officer wanted a man's wife, he would send the husband to Norfolk Island.

Old Jones killed three men in a fortnight at the saw by overwork. We used to be taken in large parties to raise a tree; when the body of the tree was raised, Old Jones would call some men away—then more; the men were bent double—they could not bear it—they fell—the tree on one or two, killed on the spot. 'Take him away; put him in the ground!' There was no more about it.

After seven years I got my liberty, and then started working about for a living where I could get it. I stowed myself away on board the *Barrington*, bound to Norfolk Island, with eighteen others; it was not a penal settlement then. Governor King was there. I had food plenty. I was overseer of the Governor's garden. Afterwards I went to live with old D'Arcy Wentworth, and a better master never lived in the world. Little Billy Wentworth, the great lawyer, has often been carried in my arms.

Old D'Arcy wanted me to take charge of his Homebush property, but I took to the river, worked up and down the Hawkesbury till I saved money to buy old Brown's farm at Pitt Town. No man worked harder than I have done. I have about me one thousand pounds ready cash. I have given that farm of forty acres to my son Joseph, and three other farms and about five hundred head of cattle; and about the same to my other son.

We are never without a chest of tea in the house; we use two in the year. I have paid £40 for a chest of tea in this colony. Tea is a great comfort.

JOSEPH SMITH

91

QUEEN OF THE HUNTER VALLEY

Much of the site of the city of Maitland, New South Wales, was at one time known as Molly Morgan's Plains. The fabulous Molly Morgan was a ratcatcher's daughter, twice convicted in England and sentenced to transportation to Australia, who died a wealthy woman with the local title of Queen of the Hunter Valley.

Born in Shropshire, Molly Jones was a pert, rosy-cheeked country lass when she married William Morgan, a wheelwright and carpenter; she bore him two children. She was already the mother of a child whose father, a well-to-do farmer, refused to marry her. To provide a little extra for the struggling family, Molly succumbed to the temptation of stealing a few shillings' worth of hempen yarn, but her pilfering was detected and she was brought to trial and sentenced to transportation for five years.

Although she sailed for Botany Bay aboard the hell-ship *Neptune*, one of the vessels of the Second Fleet, Molly Morgan's good looks and easy virtue gained her many privileges and she endured little of the sufferings of other convicts. The officers found her attractive enough to provide her with extra rations and accommodation separate from the others. Even on arrival in New South Wales the merry-eyed Molly saw her prison guards vying for her favours. It was not long before she was transferred to Parramatta and practically a free agent.

Three years after her arrival in the colony her husband, William Morgan, came with a new batch of prisoners transported also for stealing. Because of his good behaviour William was allowed to live with Molly, but he soon raised objections to his wife's flirtations with soldier friends. This was a handicap to the saucy wench, and she decided to escape from the environment. Offering herself as mistress to Captain Locke of the whaler *Resolution*, on condition that he take her back to England, the proposition was accepted. Locke found her so pleasing on the voyage that, when his vessel arrived in England, he offered her a permanent home on the *Resolution* as his companion. She declined and, after collecting her children from relatives who were looking after them, moved to Plymouth where she worked as a seamstress.

A prosperous brass founder, Thomas Mares, proposed marriage to Molly and, although she had a husband working out his sentence in far-off Australia, she accepted. The 'marriage' was happy enough in its early stages, but following a quarrel Molly set fire to Mares' home and it was burnt to the ground. Infuriated, Mares called in the police, but the arsonist had escaped to London. There she was caught and at the Croydon Quarter Sessions on 10th October 1803 was sentenced for the second time to transportation.

Fortunately for this lucky prisoner she still had good looks and a much admired figure, so it is not surprising that in a short time she was the holder of a ticket-of-leave. She was fortunate, too, inasmuch that her rightful husband, William Morgan, on his release bothered her not at all but quietly disappeared from the scene. Molly, with the help of a 'protector', a member of the Parramatta garrison, acquired a few acres of land and some horses and cattle.

Prosperity came quickly. Her herds increased so rapidly that, when puzzled officials investigated, they found that many of the beasts were ones reported as stolen. Her freedom lost, the incorrigible Molly was sent to the Coal River convict camp. Once again her charms came to her rescue and, although now in her forties, she dazzled the military men in this womanless penal outpost, who treated her more like a guest than a prisoner. Another ticket-of-leave was soon forthcoming.

Molly was more than ever determined to amass riches, and to do so quickly, but in a more or less legitimate enterprise. She decided, too, to remain in the Hunter River district where she had many men friends and admirers. Cedar-getters and settlers were moving into the fertile valley, and Molly Morgan opened a rough grog shanty for the thirsty newcomers as well as the troops and coalminers in the newly discovered coalfields. The slab and bark shanty was well patronised, and about 1818 Molly opened an inn at Wallis Plains on the present site of Maitland. Her hostelry, the Angel Inn, stood opposite where the post office now is and proved a magnet for the increasing population of the prosperous district. The buxom, but still fascinating proprietress was the toast of the town. She amassed riches enough to be considered one of the wealthiest persons in the colony, and the district in which she lived, Wallis Plains, was much better known as Molly Morgan's Plains. Here she bought up large blocks of river frontage land and all the area that now comprises the main business centre of West Maitland.

Governor Brisbane so admired her success that he gave her the use of convict gangs to clear her land. Despite the fact that she was still legally married, she went through another 'marriage' ceremony with Thomas Hunt, a handsome young garrison soldier. Yet even in her sixties she remained sprightly and shapely and always a shrewd and clever business woman. Her business acumen did not harden a 'heart of gold', and she was renowned and respected for great kindness and humanity. On one occasion she made a wild non-stop ride to Sydney in a last-minute attempt to plead with the Governor to spare the lives of some convicts sentenced to be executed for stealing fruit from an orchard. Her intercession saved them from the gallows. Little wonder that Molly Morgan was revered as the 'Queen of the Hunter Valley'. Before her death in 1833 she had subdivided her land and sold it in small blocks for business premises and residential sites, and had retired to her two-hundred-acre farm at Anvil Creek, near Greta.

THE KING OF NEW ZEALAND

Australia has seen some very odd people in its comparatively brief history, but none much odder than Charles, Baron de Thierry, self-styled King of New Zealand. He claimed to have purchased that country and the right to the title of Sovereign Chief for the payment of thirty-six axes. The Baron recruited his first subjects from among Sydney citizens when he passed through Sydney in 1837 on the way to take over his 'kingdom'. And it was from Sydney that the Baron sent his first address 'To the White People of New Zealand'.

'I go to govern within the bounds of my own territories, but I neither go as an invader or a despot. You will find in me a brother and a friend who will be proud of your advice and co-operation in legislative matters, and who, without claiming an unwilling service from you, will preside over you as guardian of your safety and prosperity.

'Believe me, I am not unmindful of your necessities. I am bringing with me a considerable number of respectable families who will add to your society and increase your feeling of security. Included will be a surgeon who will provide medical attention to the poor of both races. Competent agriculturalists will give advice; also mechanics and teachers . . . .'

Along with this proclamation to the white settlers, Baron de Thierry sent another to the Maori chiefs. It concluded as follows: 'To all chiefs who shall enter into treaty with me and engage to live in peace with other tribes, and with the whites, I will give occasional bounties, and will raise them to a respectable rank in society. Judge me by my works, as the tree is judged by its fruits.'

Baron de Thierry's early interest in New Zealand came about largely by chance. Though his title was French, he was born in England. His father had fled the Revolution and had settled in Somerset. There Charles grew up and studied at Cambridge University. While at Cambridge he became friends with two young Maori chiefs who had been brought to England by the missionary Thomas Kendall to assist with the work of preparing the first grammar of the Maori language. The young de Thierry was much taken with them, and even more with the stories Kendall had to tell of the country from which they came. He had dreams of a great colonising adventure, and evidently Kendall was impressed with the idea.

At any rate it was arranged that Kendall should take thirty-six

English axes with him to New Zealand and, in treaty with the chiefs, buy for the young Baron all the land he could. The 'deeds' to the land—many thousands of acres—were sent to the Baron in 1822, shortly after Kendall's return to New Zealand.

Armed with his title to a 'kingdom', the Baron called on the Colonial Secretary, Earl Bathurst, to ask him to recommend assistance from the British Government. Outlining his plans for the colonisation of New Zealand, he suggested grants and assisted passages for immigrants. A loan of between eight and ten thousand pounds, the security for the money to be covered by his 'deeds' and repayable within three years. Earl Bathurst wasted little time with his visitor. He reminded him that New Zealand was not a possession of the Crown, and that very definitely the British Government would not be interested in his scheme.

Thus rebuked, the Baron tried out the French Government, but, other than hinting that they would have preferred to have been approached in the first instance, they did nothing. The United States was no more helpful. Undismayed, the Baron established an office in London where he received many inquiries from interested people though little in the way of practical assistance for his scheme.

But nothing could daunt Charles dreaming of his Pacific dominion. Off he went to New Zealand, via America, visiting some of the South Sea islands on the way. While at Tahiti he issued his first royal ultimatum; it was addressed to the recently appointed British Resident in New Zealand, Mr James Busby.

I am on my way to New Zealand for the purpose of establishing there a Sovereign Government, and address you as His Brittanic Majesty's Consular Agent at the Bay of Islands.

I wish to inform you of my impending arrival, having already declared my independence to Their Majesties the Kings of Great Britain and France and to the President of the United States of America ....

I have had long negotiations with the Government of Panama for permission to cut a navigable canal across the isthmus in the Gulf of Darien. A treaty has been signed by the authorities of Panama which will allow New Zealand to enjoy the property of this canal for fifty years. The canal across Panama will bring New Zealand within eighty days' sail of England.

I intend establishing a line of ships from Panama which will bring the mails from England and the West Indies to my New Zealand kingdom ...

CHARLES, BARON DE THIERRY,
Sovereign Chief of New Zealand.

Mr Busby could scarcely believe his eyes. At first he was inclined to dismiss the document as merely the brainstorm of a madman, but he reflected that such madness suggested a man likely to be productive of much mischief. Mr Busby realised that his own position was a difficult one. As British Resident he was there to protect the interests of the whalers and traders settled in this forgotten part of the world. But with his appointment the British Government had given him no adequate power to exercise such protection. His position could be described as 'a warship without guns'. He knew, moreover, that the settlers just smiled at the protection he presumed to offer them. Worse still, they disdained his authority.

James Busby suddenly thought of the printing-press he had brought with him from England and which had yet to be used. He decided to use it for the first document to be printed in New Zealand, a proclamation warning the settlers of the communication he had received from the Baron, and requesting them to resist his coming.

The British Resident announces to his countrymen that he has received from a person who styles himself, 'Charles, Baron de Thierry, Sovereign Chief of New Zealand', a formal declaration of his intention to establish an independent sovereignty in this country.

The Resident requests British settlers of all classes to use all the influence they possess to counteract the efforts of any emissaries which may arrive amongst them; and to inspire both Maori Chiefs and people with spirit of the most determined resistance to the landing of this person on their shore who comes amongst them with the avowed intention of usurping a Government over them....

In addition to this, the British Resident prepared a printed document to be signed by the Maori chiefs with whom he was in touch. It announced the unification of their country under what was described as the 'United Tribes of New Zealand' and their request that the King of England continue as parent of their infant State and protect their land from all attempts on its independence.

Mr Busby then advised the Colonial Secretary of the course he had taken, confident that such measures would be commended. Alas, Earl Bathurst did not appreciate them and regarded the British Resident as big a nuisance as the Baron. He wrote him a sarcastic letter saying that England was not at the moment needing any more colonies and that he had no right to take on his shoulders the responsibility of making the country a colony of the Crown. 'Any moves in the matter will be done from London—not by a mere representative in New Zealand.'

In the meantime the Baron could find no shipmaster in Tahiti willing to transport him and his royal court for their landing in New Zealand. He therefore took passage to Sydney and sought assistance from Governor Bourke. His Excellency gave him none, but neither did he offer any hindrance. In Sydney the Baron gathered together a motley assortment of subjects—a retinue of nearly a hundred people. Off they sailed, and on 4th November 1837 the colonising king set foot in his 'kingdom'. The landing-place was Hokianga.

And here the dream quickly faded. His friend Kendall, the missionary, had disappeared and the Maori chiefs hailed him only with derision: King Pukanva—'King unrecognised'. The 'subjects' deserted their king almost immediately. Nevertheless there were rumours that France might recognise his claims. England then sprang into action, and on 15th June 1839 the boundaries of New South Wales were extended 'to include such portions of New Zealand as the Crown might acquire.'

Unwittingly the Baron's assumption of authority was in large part responsible for the decision of the British Government to attach New Zealand to the Crown. Of course he stoutly opposed this action. In a letter which he sent to the *Sydney Gazette* he said, 'I am an Englishman at heart, but the study of my life will be to support the independence of New Zealand under some civilised ruler, and to save this fine people from the degradation and destruction which would inevitably follow its subjection to the British Crown.

Charles, Baron de Thierry, the man who aimed to be King of New Zealand, ended his days as a humble teacher of music in Auckland.

SIR JOHN ROBERTSON

A contemporary statesman of Sir Henry Parkes, and one who alternated with him for a generation as Premier of the Colony of New South Wales, was Sir John Robertson. When he was a boy, his family

owned the whole of the peninsula at Cremorne—eighty-six acres. No ferries ran to the city in those days, and unless a special boat was hired the trip home was a long and tiring journey round from Blue's Point. But young John had his own particular way of getting home. He would walk to Mrs Macquarie's Chair in the Sydney Domain, make a bundle of his clothes, tie them on his head, and swim across the harbour to Fort Denison. After a spell he would take to the water again and swim across to his home. It was one of Sydney's sights in those days to see young Robertson swimming home in the moonlight.

In his old age Sir John lived at Vaucluse, then also an isolated and far-distant part of Sydney. After Parliament adjourned, he would ride home on his white horse named Blucher. Always on cold or wet nights Sir James would call at the hotel at the corner of Bathurst and Elizabeth streets to fortify himself for the long journey. He invariably ordered three pints of rum. One he drank himself, another he gave to the horse, and the third pint was poured equally into his riding-boots to keep the rheumatics out.

Robertson was an ultra-picturesque personality. His long, silvery mane of hair and beard framed an aggressive, hawk-like face, and the courageous eyes that looked through you did not know how to falter or express fear. His commanding voice never cared a straw what it uttered. Whatever came into his mind to utter was expressed loudly and without compromise to all who might be within range.

Whilst he was Premier, a deputation representing Victoria came to see him.

'Victoria? What the devil do I care for Victoria!' exploded Sir John. 'A cow country to the south of the Murray inhabited by starving savages!'

On another occasion a deputation interviewed him from an outback township that had been promised telegraphic communication with Sydney. Sir John kept his temper whilst he patiently explained that the PMG's Department was short of the necessary telegraph wire. But when the leader of the deputation kept insisting that there must be some way out of the difficulty, the Premier smote his desk with a heavy fist. 'Confound it, you idiots! D'yer think I'm a so-and-so *spider* that I can *spin* ruddy telegraph wire out of my blanky body?'

The prize story relates to the occasion when Sir John absent-mindedly walked into the harbour. One morning he strode from his home on to the ferry wharf reading his newspaper and acknowledging the respectful greetings of friends and neighbours waiting for the ferry. He walked right over the pier's end into the harbour!

There was a rush of rescuers. To their astonishment, the old fellow disdained their efforts to fish him out. He swam away from the ferry wharf and emerged, dripping and fierce, in the middle of the beach. There he was met by an expostulating leading resident of the district who wailed, 'Oh, Sir John! Sir John! You shouldn't have done that!'

'And why the hades shouldn't I?'

'Oh, Sir John, a shark might have got you!'

'Indeed! Well I'd a ruddy sight sooner a shark had got me than have you flaming fools sticking your blanky boat-hooks in my crimson carcass!'

When Sir John Robertson died he was widely mourned. He was accorded a State funeral, and public subscriptions erected a fine statue to his memory. Cardinal Moran said of him, 'The veteran who has passed away had not among his compeers, during his long and eventful public career, one more remarkable in the building up and preservation of those rights which he believed to be so essential to the greatness of Australia. None more faithfully served the State than he.'

ROSE DE FREYCINET

To begin with, everything about Rose de Freycinet was remarkable. The twenty-three-year-old traveller wore a low-necked, hip-waisted white muslin dress with a blue sash, and her short, curling hair was held by a blue band ornamented with two tall feathers. Under one arm was tucked a guitar. Hardly a nautical outfit, but this was part of Madame de Freycinet's wardrobe on the epic voyage that gave her the distinction of being the first Frenchwoman to sail around the world, and the first white woman to set foot in Western Australia.

On her world voyage Rose de Freycinet kept a journal, and its contents while giving a faithful account of her impressions of her travels reveal the writer as a charming personality, gentle, sometimes naive, and essentially feminine. Especially interesting are the many pencil and watercolour sketches in the journal made by members of her husband's expedition. One coloured sketch depicts the French camp at Shark Bay in Western Australia with Madame de Freycinet seated at the entrance to her flagged tent. When the burning sands made walking unpleasant, she spent most of her time sewing, or reading, or playing the guitar.

Captain Louis de Freycinet first visited Western Australia in the early years of the nineteenth century on a French scientific expedition under the command of Commodore Baudin. A few years later de Freycinet was given command of the *Uranie* to undertake further scientific investigations. He had been married two years when the *Uranie* left Toulon in September 1817, and he was accompanied by his wife—unofficially. Indeed, she came aboard as a stowaway.

Rose de Freycinet's exciting adventures, recorded in her journal, begin with her boarding the vessel at Toulon shortly after midnight on 4th September 1817 with 'dear Louis'. She was disguised in boy's clothes, and her hair cut short, and she confesses that she was terrified that she might be discovered by the port authorities and sent ashore.

No sooner did the *Uranie* leave Toulon than the vessel was battered by a gale, and Rose was miserably sick. To add to her troubles, an Algerian corsair was seen following the *Uranie*, and the nervous woman was convinced that it was a pirate vessel intent on opening fire on them. She feared that in the event of capture she would be sold into slavery. However, the gale eventually abated, the corsair disappeared from view, and the young traveller settled down to shipboard life.

The *Uranie* visited Brazil, the Cape of Good Hope, and Mauritius, and sighted the coast of Western Australia on 12th September 1818, just about a year after leaving France. The vessel anchored at Shark Bay 'in the midst of a prodigious number of whales sporting in the waters and spouting brilliant jets of water into the air. Sometimes the whales struck the *Uranie* with their enormous tails.' The journal records that Captain de Freycinet's first undertaking was to send a boat to Dirk Hartog Island to search for the copper plate left there by Vlamingh in 1697.

Another party was equipped to make geographical observations along the coast. Rose accompanied Louis to the mainland and was startled to see a group of Aborigines armed with spears and clubs. She hid in fear behind her husband, but the 'savages' made no attempt to attack them and soon left. 'The heat was intense, but we had lunch ashore under the protection of a canvas awning. A delicious meal was made from the wonderful oysters collected around the rocks.'

Rose de Freycinet spent several days on shore, but records that she found little to admire because of the heat and 'the monotonous nature of the country'. A ship's party went into the interior to study the Aborigines, but they lost themselves and were two days without food or water before they regained the camp.

After spending ten days at Shark Bay, the *Uranie* continued her voyage round the north of Australia, turned south to the little settlement at Sydney Cove, and then across the Pacific and round Cape Horn. Shortly after leaving the Cape, the vessel was wrecked and, although she was beached without the loss of lives, some of the scientific data and specimens were damaged or ruined. Members of the expedition eventually returned to France in a whaling vessel. Rose de Freycinet died from cholera in France a few years later. Cape Rose on the eastern side of Peron Peninsula, Western Australia, perpetuates the memory of the woman who braved storms, shipwreck and many perils of the unknown to remain by the side of her young husband.

THE PRINCE OF AUSTRALIA
One of the best-known and admired men in the Sydney of the 1820s

was Captain John Piper, the 'Prince of Australia'. His great popularity is indicated by the repeated use of his name on the map, near and far. Piper is commemorated in the naming of a river in Tasmania, a cape and a group of islands in the Northern Territory, and several localities near Sydney.

A Scotsman, born in Ayrshire, he came to the colony as an ensign with the New South

Wales Corps in 1792 and took up duty on Norfolk Island. While there he married Mary Ann Shears, daughter of a convict, who bore him a large family. Promoted to the rank of lieutenant, he eventually returned to the mainland where, in 1800, he received the local rank of captain. Piper was friendly with John Macarthur and acted as his second in a duel with Colonel William Paterson. For this he was arrested, together with Macarthur, and tried by court martial, but was acquitted.

Piper was made naval officer for Port Jackson, an office which developed into a combination of being in charge of the customs house, harbour trust, and water police. He collected the harbour dues and customs duties, and was paid a commission of five per cent on all monies collected. With Sydney increasing rapidly in importance as a port, his fortunes rose rapidly. Added to this, he was given various grants of land round the foreshores of Sydney Harbour—Vaucluse, Woollahra, Neutral Bay—and he built a mansion on the beautiful promontory now known as Point Piper, which became famous for its social life.

Piper revealed not the slightest hint of Scottish thrift, but entertained on an extraordinarily lavish scale. He spent a fortune on his racing-stables and aquatic sports, and was generous to his relatives and those less fortunate than himself. A good sportsman, a horse-lover, and generally a 'good fellow', he was lax as a tax-collector. As President of the Bank of New South Wales he granted his friends, according to Governor Darling, 'great and improvident accommodation', falling from financial grace to the extent of having to sell his properties (including Vaucluse House) to meet the monetary claims made upon him.

Dismissed from office, Piper's many friends rallied to his aid, and enough was saved from the chaos of his affairs to make a fresh start on a property of two thousand acres near Bathurst. There he enjoyed many happy days and was honoured by a visit from Governor Darling and his wife in 1819. If he had been able to live within his income, his station property might have been very successful. It certainly gave him and his family a good return for many years. Alas, Piper began to resume his former extravagant mode of living, and the depression of 1844 caused him to lose the property. He moved into a small holding—

Westbourne—in the Bathurst district and died there in 1851 at the age of seventy-eight.

Piper's misfortunes largely arose from his lack of business sense and his inability to repulse spongers. But it was also said of him that he was 'too noble-minded to desire to make a fortune from the labour of the settler, the plunder of the soldier, or from the sweat of the convict's brow'.

THE FLYING PIEMAN

On an early September morning of 1848 the township of Windsor, in New South Wales, was agog with excitement as local settlers and their wives, district officials, ticket-of-leave men, and soldiers made their way to the mail-coach terminal. Already a group had gathered round the coach-driver, watching him grease every movable part of the sturdy vehicle, oiling the harness, and polishing the metalwork. An assistant was grooming his horses to perfection. The arrival and departure of the mail for Sydney were always the main events of the week, but never had there been such a stir as on this day.

Standing by the coach was a tall, fair man whose magnificent physique belied his age of forty years or more. This was the famed Flying Pieman, the phenomenon of the sporting world whose pedestrian feats were already legendary. Today he was to race the coach to Sydney, a distance of thirty miles or thereabouts. The splendidly proportioned athlete, glowing with health, nodded and chatted to well-wishers and supporters, receiving the major portion of the crowd's plaudits.

The signal came for the hour of departure. With the crack of the whip the horses jumped into their collars, and the Flying Pieman bounded away with long effortless strides. For the first few miles the contestants were followed by a string of cheering spectators in vehicles and on horseback, anxious to see as much as they could of the historic supremacy between horses and man, but they gradually thinned out and eventually gave up the hot pace being set. That afternoon in Sydney a crowd of citizens gathered at the Obelisk in Macquarie Place awaiting the outcome of the strange contest. Early in the evening a great cheer went up as the human deer was seen striding down the road to the finishing-line. They were still showering him with congratulations when, seven minutes later, the coach arrived drawn by foam-lathered horses with an unhappy driver shaking his head in bewilderment.

That same month the Flying Pieman set out to walk 192 miles in 48 hours, the conditions being that he was not to stop for a minute. He was watched by three men in relays, one of whom kept tally, another attended to the fire, while the third slept. He accomplished the task and covered the distance in 46 hours 30 minutes.

In February 1848, at Singleton, New South Wales, he covered 500 half-miles in 500 consecutive half-hours. At Dungog he wheeled a barrow a mile, took fifty flying leaps, picked up fifty stones a yard apart, ran backwards for half a mile, and after that carried an eighty-pound live goat a mile and a half in twelve minutes. On another occasion he carried a big pole and beat the Brisbane to Ipswich mail-coach by an hour on the road. He walked from Sydney to Parramatta (a distance of fifteen miles) and back twice a day for six consecutive days. Often he would carry a live sheep on his back, or a boy on his shoulders, with incredible fleetness of foot.

His real name was William King, and when not engaged on his flying feats he made pies, 'kidney, pork, mutton or apple pies—all hot!' King was the eldest son of a paymaster of accounts at the Treasury in Whitewall, London. He was intended for the Church but, unfortunately for his parents' ambitions, he preferred the sporting field to the pulpit. Before coming to New South Wales in 1838, he was a clerk in the Treasury office at the Tower of London.

After his arrival here he became a schoolmaster at Sutton Forest, near Bong Bong, an appointment given him by Archbishop Broughton. Later he became a tutor, and finally, before completely embracing professional pedestrianism, he was a barman at the Hope and Anchor tavern in Sydney. Toward the end of his life he developed into one of the best-known street characters of early Sydney; he always wore a top hat with coloured streamers, and carried a walking-stick to which ribbons were attached. It was said of him that he received regular remittances from England, but he died a pauper in the Liverpool asylum for old men in 1874.

COLE OF THE BOOK ARCADE

Edward William Cole, founder of Cole's Book Arcade, Melbourne, was one of those extraordinary individuals who would have made a personal success in any circumstances. When he died in 1918, Melbourne lost one of its most picturesque personalities. He was born in Kent, England, in 1832, and received little education.

At the age of twenty Cole migrated to Victoria, where he spent some time in various occupations on the goldfields. In 1865 he opened a bookshop at the Eastern Market, Melbourne, with a stock of six hundred volumes which gave him a modest turnover of £3 a week. Living very frugally, Cole spent every penny he could in buying fresh stock, and his business began to prosper. He gradually became lessee of the whole of the market, a large part of which he sublet to small stallholders. To supplement his scanty education he read a great deal, and he began to publish some of his own writings, including a religious work and poems of mediocre quality.

In 1874 Cole opened his first book arcade, and a few years later founded another book business near the Melbourne General Post Office. Members of the public were invited to walk through the arcade, to spend as much time as they liked browsing through books or even reading them in their entirety. Cole was full of ideals regarded as fantastic in those days. He believed in the brotherhood of man, the federation of the world, and such like. He compiled a number of popular books, of which *Cole's Funny Picture Book*, *Cole's Fun Doctor* and *Cole's Book on Love* were enormously successful, their sales running into hundreds of thousands.

It is interesting to note that in 1964 the Libraries Board of South Australia issued a facsimile edition of Cole's sixpenny publication, *Thatcher's Colonial Songs* ('Forming a Complete History of the Early Diggings', as the cover states). The only difference in Cole's sixpenny publication and the 1964 copy of it was the price. The facsimile edition sold at twenty-five shillings. Charles Thatcher was a well-known writer and singer of popular and topical songs at the Victorian goldfields in the middle of the nineteenth century. The songs, set to favourite tunes, were described by a contemporary as giving 'a much better idea of life at the goldfields than most of the elaborately written works upon them do'.

Long before the aeroplane came, Cole had offered £1,000 to the first aviator to land in front of his shop. And what a curious bookshop it was, with his cages of monkeys, parrots, a band playing every afternoon in the second-hand department, and ideals! Cole's bookshop was an exciting place to work in. Mr Cole used to get temperamental and regularly each week would dismiss most of the employees. However Mr Cole would re-engage them the same day, and everyone would be pacified until the next week. Nevertheless most of his employees stayed there throughout his long life, and his establishment had a considerable effect on the culture of Melbourne.

THE AUTOGRAPH KING

Digger S. B. Williams was known throughout the 1st AIF as the Autograph King. His remarkable collections of two thousand signatures contained many famous names, including forty-two representatives of royalty. The autographs of kings, queens, presidents, an ex-Kaiser, the ex-Crown Prince of Germany, Ludendorff, Litvinov, and Stalin were to be seen in his book.

Lunching one day at the Anzac Buffet, Victoria Street, London, Williams encountered an old mate. There were about four hundred Diggers in the buffet at the time.

'Hullo, Williams, you old so-and-so!' was his friend's greeting. 'How's your autograph collection these days? Have you got George to sign the book yet?'

'If you mean Lloyd George, yes.'

'No, no, KING George at Buckingham Palace!'

'Well, it's funny you should mention it,' mused Williams, 'because I'm going to the palace this afternoon to get his Majesty's signature.'

'Struth!' exclaimed his mate. Looking across to a crowd of soldiers he called out, 'Hey, Digs, what do you know! Williams is going up to Buckingham Palace this arvo to get King George to sign his autograph book!'

There were derisive cries of 'They'll toss him out with bayonets', and suchlike.

'Leave it to me, boys!' Digger Williams smilingly replied. 'I tell you what: if you're here this time tomorrow, I'll show you the signature not only of King George, but of Queen Mary!'

Lord Kitchener's death had been announced at just about this time, and London was in a state of tension. Cabinet Ministers, generals, admirals, all were being closely guarded by the secret service. Buckingham Palace was especially under strict surveillance; the guards had been increased at the gates, and close scrutiny was maintained of all persons approaching the environs of the palace.

It was considered an utter impossibility to get through without authority, but nothing daunted Williams. He had taken the precaution of placing his large autograph book in an extra large and impressive envelope addressed to 'Lord Stamfordham, Private Secretary to His Majesty'. With the book was a letter inside the envelope asking Lord Stamfordham to aid the bearer in getting the signatures of their Majesties the King and Queen.

And so the super-optimist approached the palace gates. Armed sentries were marching up and down both sides of the iron railings. A group of policemen were in charge of a sergeant who, on seeing Williams approach called out, 'What do you want?'

'I have a letter, sir, for Lord Stamfordham.'

'Show me. H'mm. Constable, escort this man to the office.' Within a few minutes Williams had been quickly passed from one official to another, each of whom scanned the important looking envelope, not daring to open it or inquire into the nature of its contents. It was presumed that this Australian soldier was carrying a secret document from his commander.

When Williams was eventually handed over to Lord Stamfordham's own private secretary, the latter personally escorted him into the presence of his chief.

'You have a letter for me? Thank you, take a seat. What the dickens is all this? Why ...it's...it's an autograph book!'

Williams took a deep breath. 'Forgive me, sir. It's a very special favour that I'm asking. May I leave my autograph book with you? I'm sure that, if you will be kind enough to show it to their Majesties, they will graciously sign it.'

Lord Stamfordham looked in astonishment at Williams before he replied. 'It's incredible, simply incredible! And to think the palace is being doubly guarded these days! Scotland Yard won't believe it when I tell them. Why you, you might have been an assassin! Do you know that you're the first person in the history of Buckingham Palace to gain entry into their Majesties' residence solely to obtain the royal autographs? Moreover, you should very well know that they *never* sign autograph books....I don't know whether to call the guards and have you thrown into the Tower, or to recommend you for a VC...Leave the book. I'll see what I can do about it.'

'Thank you, sir.'

Great was the joy of Williams when, only a few hours later, there came to the hostel where he was staying whilst on leave a King's messenger bearing the autograph book, with the signatures of the King and Queen!

WOMEN ON THE MAP

On a plane trip returning from Alice Springs one of the passengers asked, 'Who was the Alice of Alice Springs?' Having done some research work for a *Sydney Morning Herald* article concerning women on the Australian map, I had no difficulty in supplying the answer.

The Alice, of Alice Springs, was the wife of Sir Charles Todd, who was primarily responsible for the building of the Overland Telegraph line. He said the proudest moment of his life was when Alice Bell agreed to marry him and go with him to Australia, and he felt almost as proud when he sat on the ground at Central Mount Stuart on the very cold night of 22nd August 1872, and with a pocket instrument spoke to both Darwin and Adelaide.

Discoverers of precious watering-places in Australia's arid lands seem to have had a predilection for naming them after their women-folk: Emily Springs, Maggie Springs, Lady Edith Springs (the latter was changed at the request of Lady Edith to that of her family name, Dalhousie), and Charlotte Waters. An ethereal Byronic romance is reflected in the placid pool of Central Australia's Charlotte Waters. This desert oasis, the waters of which have never run dry, lies just beyond the northern border of South Australia, on the Overland Telegraph route.

The Charlotte, of Charlotte Waters, was Lady Charlotte Bacon—the Ianthe ('Love's image') to whom Byron dedicated his masterpiece, *Childe Harold*. Sixth daughter of the Earl of Oxford, she was only thirteen years old when Byron first saw her. Deeply moved by her tender, blossoming beauty, the twenty-six-year-old poet ('my years already doubly numbered thine') penned the famous dedication verse to his just completed work. He also commissioned her portrait by William Westall, RA, who in his youth had sailed the coasts of Australia as artist with Captain Matthew Flinders. The engraving has accompanied the poem in all editions.

A brave, beautiful and intellectual woman, a dashing rider, hers was a long and adventurous life. At the age of nineteen Charlotte married Major-General Anthony Bacon, a hero of Waterloo and the Spanish Wars, where she shared with him the perils and hardships of the Siege of Oporto, 1832-5, She arrived in South Australia in the 1860s with three of her children, but after some years returned to England, where she died in 1880 at the age of seventy-nine. Descendants are still living in South Australia.

One of her sons, Harley Bacon, was a member of the Central Australian expedition in the building of the Overland Telegraph line. In 1871, when the three surveyors, Woods, McMinn, and Knuckey, came to the place now known as Charlotte Waters, Knuckey wrote in his diary: 'I jumped off my horse and tasted the water. You can imagine my delight when I found it fresh.... We solemnly filled our pannikins and I named the "waters" Charlotte, after Lady Charlotte Bacon, sixth daughter of the Earl of Oxford.'

Great was my surprise when, on a visit to the west coast settlement of Lake Wangarry, in the Port Lincoln district of South Australia, I was shown Byron's town coach, which the poet had presented to Charlotte and which she brought with her to South Australia. It was 'housed' in a tumbledown shed in the yard of a little outback pub. Despite its dilapidated appearance there was no mistaking the vehicle's beauty of line and hint of former elegance. I peered at the romantic scrolled arms and crest of Byron on one of the doors. Barely discernible was the Latin inscription, 'Crede Biron'.

How did this chariot of Apollo, once the most glorious and notorious in all London, come to rest at such an outlandish place. Mine host could not supply the answer, except to say that it was there when he took over and that when he first saw it fowls had made it into a nesting-place. Deep in the grooved cushions were several eggs!

Maggie Springs was named by explorer Gosse, discoverer of Ayers Rock, in honour of Margaret, daughter of Alexander Hay. Emily Springs commemorates the wife of a South Australian pioneer.

Among the women on Australia's map is Lady Eliza Grey, immortalised by her husband, Sir George Grey, who named Lake Eliza in her honour.

Mount Daisy Bates is a tribute to that remarkable woman who devoted her life to the care of the Aborigines.

The Countess Diamantina Roma, a descendant of an ancient Venetian family and the wife of Queensland Governor Bowen, has the triple distinction of being honoured in the naming of the town of Roma, Mount Diamantina, and the Diamantina River.

There must have been some ardent feminists among pioneers of the Kimberley country in Western Australia. Twelve of its peaks are named after women: Mount Nelly, Mount Amy, Mount Rose, Mount Elizabeth, Mount Agnes, Mount Beatrice, Mount Edith, Mount Dorothy, Mount Gertrude, Mount Deborah, Princess May Ranges, and the Caroline Ranges. In the same area is the Margaret River and the Victoria River. Truly, a woman's world!

One of the few Aboriginal women honoured with a placename is the brave young woman, Narrabeen. The first white man to live in the district now named after her was Captain Reynolds, a military man who came out in the First Fleet. After his retirement he built his home there for himself and family. The captain was very friendly with a tribe of Aborigines who lived near by. Especially did he like their chief, Yowal.

Some desperate convicts escaped from Sydney and began to roam the bush. They were led by a cunning criminal nicknamed Big Mick. The latter came across the homestead of Reynolds and remembered that the captain had ordered him to be flogged on one occasion after a convict mutiny. Big Mick called his gang together and outlined a plan for the killing of every member of the homestead.

Unknown to the criminals, Narrabeen, Yowal's daughter, was watching them through the thick bushes. Silently the girl stole away and told her father. Yowal immediately made his way to the homestead and warned his friend.

The captain and his family barricaded themselves in and got out their firearms. Mrs Reynolds put the baby in its cot and took her place alongside her husband and thirteen-year old son, each of them with a rifle. Nevertheless, the attackers so outnumbered them that during the raid all the members of the homestead were killed.

Meanwhile Narrabeen was making her way to Sydney for help. It was twenty miles away, mostly through thick bush. Eventually she arrived back from the long journey leading a detachment of soldiers from the garrison. Though they were too late to save the Reynolds family, they were in time to capture Big Mick and all his murderous gang.

THE WILD WHITE MAN

When William Buckley, the ex-convict who escaped from the Port Phillip settlement and spent thirty-two years with the wild Aborigines of Victoria, returned to civilisation he was pardoned. Later he was given a job in the Tasmanian Public Service. When he reached his seventieth birthday, on 10th October 1850, he was retired from his job. The following day the *Hobart Town Advertiser* sent a special journalist, Mr Harry Greatorex, to interview Buckley.

The journalist said that, on arriving at Buckley's cottage at New Town, Mrs Buckley and her daughter, Rose, met him at the front gate and escorted him with words of welcome up the marigold-edged path to the house. There he found Mr Buckley with an old clay pipe in his mouth reclining in a comfortable armchair on the back verandah.

'Can't get up,' he said. 'Touch of the rheumatiz this morning. Must be getting old.'

'Well, now that you've retired,' Mr Greatorex began.

'Yes,' he replied slowly and contemplatively, 'I'm a has-been; I was seventy yesterday. Now I've got nothing to do except sit here and smoke and think over the olden times.'

'Oh, don't be so gloomy, William,' interrupted Mrs Buckley. 'Why

you'll be able to enjoy the rest of your life without any worry.'

The journalist asked Buckley to tell him something of his life as a boy.

'It's such a long time ago,' he murmured, taking the pipe out of his mouth and tapping down the tobacco with a great thumb. 'Why! I was born before Cap'n Phillip came out to Botany Bay! Think of that! I'm an Englishman, I am, come from Cheshire. Ever been in Cheshire?'

Mr Greatorex shook his head.

'Father was a farmer, used to grow turnips, mostly. I had nine brothers and sisters. Haven't heard a word from 'em for years. Most of them dead by now, I suppose.'

'Now, William,' interposed Mrs Buckley, 'Mr Greatorex wants to hear about you, not your relatives.'

'Well, I went to live with my grandfather in Abbey Close. He was a bricklayer, a good one too. Belonged to the Guild. I was his apprentice, but I didn't like it. Couldn't abide climbing ladders. So, when I was nineteen, I cleared out. What do you think I did? Enlisted as a soldier. Joined the King's Own Regiment. Ten guineas was the bounty—a right good sum in those days. I spent it mostly on the gals,' added Buckley with a chuckle.

'William, please!' Mrs Buckley chided.

'Did you see any active service?' the journalist asked.

'Did I what!' He sparked up at once. 'Look at this! Here's where a Frenchie's bullet went right through my hand when we were fighting in Holland.'

'A nasty scar. How long were you in the army?'

'Best part of five years. I was number one in the front rank, too,' he said proudly. 'I'm six feet six inches tall, I am.'

'I can see you must have been a young giant. What made you give up the military life?' The *Advertiser's* representative knew that Buckley had come out to Botany Bay as a guest of Her Majesty's Government, but he wanted his own version.

Misfortune,' he responded. 'Misfortune, and a couple of bad companions. There were some pretty bad eggs in the army in those days, Morgan and O'Neill were their names. Morgan was a rat-faced little Cockney. O'Neill came from Cork. They robbed a shop, an old woman's draper shop. All I did was to help them dispose of the swag. "Receiving stolen goods", the Bow Street runner called it. The old beak was against us. "Guilty," he said, and next day I was sent to the hulks at Woolwich.'

'How long were you there, Mr Buckley?' He was easy to interview, as the cockles of his memory warmed up.

'Best part of a year, lumping stones and muck onto the Thames embankment in a wheelbarrow all day, and eaten alive by bugs and lice and cockroaches all night.'

'But how did you manage to come to Australia?' the interviewer queried, side-tracking his penal experiences.

'My sentence was changed to transportation. Came out in the *Calcutta* with Colonel Collins to help establish the new settlement at Port Phillip. 'Twas in the year 1803, I remember. Another ship, the *Ocean*, came out with us. Three hundred convicts there were on board.

Colonel Collins, a fine old gentleman he was, he treated me well on the voyage. Made me his own personal servant.'

'How did you find conditions when you arrived?'

'Ah, that's a different story. 'Twas hell on earth. Port Phillip was all bush and we were made to work at hard labour from daylight to dark. Some of the prisoners tried to escape, but they were recaptured and given a hundred lashes each.' Mr. Greatorex wondered whether the narrator had been one of these, but kept silent. 'Even the Governor himself was fed up with the settlement, and decided to transfer it to Van Diemen's Land.'

'But you didn't go to the Derwent with him?'

'No,' he replied. 'With five other convicts I planned an escape. For weeks we collected any provisions we could, planting them in the bush. Then, just after Christmas, we made a break. One man, McGuire, was shot dead by the guards, another was captured. Four of us got clear away. We headed due north for Botany Bay. It wasn't long before we met a tribe of natives. I fired my musket, and they all ran away. One of my mates got frightened, so he went back to the settlement to give himself up.

'When all our food was eaten we made a bee-line for the coast. For a while we lived on oysters and mussels and other shellfish. Then we wandered on through the scrub. But we just couldn't get our bearings, and my two mates, Malcolm and Tom the Ganger, made up their minds to give in and return to the settlement, if they could find their way back. They were never heard of again. Probably died in the bush or were killed by the natives.'

A long pause ensued, while the old man puffed reflectively away, his thoughts far back in the distant past.

'How did you come to join the native tribes, Mr Buckley?' The interviewer had come to the crucial point of the interrogation. Immediately Buckley's eyes brightened and he became more animated.

'It's a long story. I'm a bit confused about it, too. Can't remember as well as I used to do. For weeks I must have wandered about in the bush, often starving. Once I was nearly drowned. Then I found a cave on the shore, near a good stream of fresh water and with plenty of fish and blackberry bushes. There I stayed until I looked like Robinson

Crusoe, with a long beard and ragged clothes.' He smiled at the thought.

'Then one day,' he continued, on the cliff above my cave I saw three blackfellows stark naked. So I hid for a while in a cleft of the rock. Though they all had nulla-nullas, they seemed to be pretty friendly. So I risked it and came cautiously out of hiding. They were astonished when they saw me, for they had never seen a white man before. One of them caught a lobster and gave me a bit of it. That night I stayed with them, but they were gone in the morning. For a long time after that I just wandered about, living as best I could. Sometimes I caught a possum; often I had nothing to eat except the gum that oozed out of the trees.'

'And did you see no other natives all this time?'

'Only at a distance. Then a strange thing happened. One day I found a native spear on a heap of sand. I was at the end of my tether. I felt my end had come when I fell down exhausted. But I was saved by two young gins. Accidentally these lubras came upon me and, seeing my condition, they ran away and brought back some men of their tribe. When they saw the spear in my hand, they set up a shout and began to yabber excitedly. As I found out later, they recognised the spear as that of their chief; he had died a little before and it had been laid on his grave. At once they jumped to the conclusion that I was his spirit come back to earth again in the form of a white man. He had been a very tall man and a great warrior.'

'And,' the interviewer commented, 'you filled the bill exactly.'

'Well, I was tall all right. And broad, too. They began to call me Murrangurk, which was the name of their dead chief, carried me carefully to their gunyahs, and fed me on gum water and those big, fat white tree-grubs they call witcheties. In a few days my strength began to return. Of course I couldn't talk to them except by signs.'

'Was a corroboree held in honour of your return from the grave?'

'Yes, the very first night I met them they held a corroboree to honour Murrangurk: "Go down blackfellow, jump up white fellow." I'll never forget it—all of them throwing themselves about and falling down exhausted with blood streaming from cut heads and bodies. Next day they led me away across a river, which I found out afterwards was the Barwon, and at last we reached the main camp. There must have been a hundred blacks there, men, women, and piccaninnies, and a good many mangy dogs, too.'

'Was it a permanent camp?'

'No. They never have permanent camps. This one was close to a marsh, where the women worked hard with their yam-sticks pulling up the tubers of a kind of lily. These they cooked over a fire of ashes. They tasted like sweet carrots. They were the first cooked vegetables I had eaten since my escape.' He rolled his tongue appreciatively at the thought.

'Did these other natives also believe that you were the spirit of the dead warrior?'

'They did! They all held another corroboree to welcome me home.'

'Did you eventually go "all native" like your black friends?'

'Yes, I became like one of them. I used all their weapons. Why, I can still throw a boomerang as well as any native. Rose—' turning to his daughter—'show the gentleman the boomerang I made for your mother!'

'And exactly how long did you live with the natives?'

'Thirty-two years it was, so they told me later. But I soon lost all count of time.'

'And what about women?' the journalist ventured to suggest when Mrs Buckley and Rose had retired for a few minutes to brew a dish of tea. 'Surely you didn't remain a bachelor all those long years?'

'I certainly did not!' he answered with a chuckle. 'Almost immediately I was presented with a young gin for a wife. She was pretty good to look at, plump and good tempered enough. Her name was Warnoo, meaning she was fat.'

'Did you keep her throughout your life with the natives?'

'No, I didn't. She wasn't faithful for long. One night she was carried off by some natives of another tribe. I think she wanted to go.'

'Was that the end of your love affairs?'

The old man laughed. 'Not at all! I had half a dozen other women at various times, but no children. Maybe black and white couldn't mix.'

'Tell me, Mr Buckley, did you remain with the same tribe throughout the years?'

'No. I must have wandered all over eastern Victoria and Gippsland, now with one tribe, now with another. Sometimes I spent months by myself near the sea coast' Once I had a whole year with a young gin. Then her relatives took her away, and I was alone . . . . It's a bit hazy now. I used to call her Matchimek.'

'And did you never see or hear of any white man in those thirty-two years?'

'Only a couple of times. Once some natives told me that there was a ship at anchor off the coast, and that a boat's crew had landed on the beach. I rushed down to the shore. Sure enough, there was a ship. I stood on the beach shouting and making signs to her. But I found I had forgotten my native tongue. English words wouldn't come. A sentry even aimed a gun at me. Burnt black as I was, and naked like the natives, I suppose I must have appeared just another blackfellow to him. I watched the seamen get into the boat and return to the ship, which then sailed away.'

'How did you feel?' the journalist asked sympathetically.

'Terribly disappointed, but also curious. I went down to the scrub near the beach, and there found a newly made grave. A little wooden cross gave the name of a seaman, Thomas Woodruffe it was. I remember it because Woodruffe was my mother's maiden name. Later I heard from some of the natives that a second boat's crew had landed in another bay with two prisoners whom they tied up to a tree and shot.'

'And how were you finally rescued?' Mr Greatorex asked the wiry old giant. He felt he was beginning to tire.

'Well, one day,' he said, 'a party of young tribesmen came to me excitedly and showed me some coloured handkerchiefs they said had been given them by some white men who had come ashore from a ship, and who had two tents and plenty of goods and food with them. Straight away I rushed down to the coast. But when I got there I was too confused to go up to the tents, so I sat down on a log to compose myself. Then I made signs to my fellow white men. Some of them came up to me. Of course they had no idea who I was. I tried to speak, but again no English words would come. Then one of them offered me some food, saying, "Bread." Immediately a cloud appeared to lift from my brain. I kept saying, "Bread! Bread!" Other words came and I was able to tell them I was a white man. They took me to their tents, gave me English food—biscuits, tea, bullybeef—and did I enjoy them!'

'Did you tell them your early history?'

'No. I was still afraid of the law. When I showed them my initials, W.B.—look here they are tattooed on my arm—they took me for a shipwrecked sailor.'

'Who were these people who rescued you, Mr Buckley?'

'They said they were the advance guard of a group of settlers led by John Batman. He was due to arrive from Launceston in a few days to open up the country round Port Phillip. They told me the date was then July 1835.'

'And what then?'

'Oh, I stayed with the newcomers. When Batman discovered that I spoke the native language, he asked me to join his party as guide and interpreter. Soon I was decked out in English clothes, and damned

uncomfortable they were at first, especially the boots.'

'What about your fear of the law?'

'I had nothing to worry about. When Mr Wedge, Batman's surveyor, returned to Van Diemen's Land he told the whole story to Governor Arthur. I had confided in Mr Wedge, because he was such a good friend to me. Anyway, Governor Arthur at once granted me a full pardon. Mother,' he called, 'show the gentleman Governor Arthur's pardon.'

'And what have you done since your return?'

'Well, first I stayed with John Batman and Mr Wedge and helped them on their bush expeditions. Then, when Captain Lonsdale came over as Superintendent of the new settlement at Port Phillip, he made me a trooper. But I didn't like the job of hunting down the natives. You see, they were my friends. So I gave it up and came back here to Hobart, where I've been ever since.'

'I believe you got a good reception.'

The old man's interest was renewed. 'There certainly was a crowd waiting at the wharf to see me. Some thought I was a kind of hero, others expected to see a wild man of the woods. Why, a showman offered me a job to appear on the stage, at a good fee too. But I wouldn't take it. I worked for a while as a storekeeper; later I was given the job as gatekeeper of the Female Home. That's the position from which I have just retired.'

'And Mrs Buckley?'

'We've been married ten years, and very happily married. My wife was a widow. Her first husband was speared by the blacks when travelling from Melbourne to Sydney.'

He turned to his buxom spouse. 'Mr Greatorex wants you in the story, too, so I'm just giving him your good points.'

She smiled in appreciation, and said, 'Better leave me out. William is big enough for your story. But don't forget to tell your readers that he's got a government pension, a pound a week for life: not very much, but we'll manage.'

In 1856, six years after the *Hobart Town Advertiser* interview, William Buckley died from injuries received in a buggy accident. He is buried in the graveyard of St George's Church.

Any ability Buckley may have had seems to have atrophied during his long career as a wild white man, for he could give little information about the habits of the Aborigines; his most sensible remark was a suggestion that there should be no interference with the natives' way of life and customs.

WHITE WOMEN WITH NATIVES

A relic of one of Australia's mystery wrecks is a grave in the old cemetery at Cooktown, North Queensland, with a headstone bearing the inscription: 'Here lies the Normanby Woman.' The Normanby Woman, as she was called, was a mysterious white woman who, in 1886, was found living with a tribe of natives in the wild and little-known country of Cape York Peninsula. She was first seen by a young Englishman, Charles Jodrell, when he was out searching for horses. Although naked like the rest of the Aborigines, she was not dark skinned, merely suntanned, and she had fair hair and light grey eyes. After her capture later by a police party she was found to have a skin whiter and fairer than any white woman in the district. She was about thirty years of age and had been rescued by the natives when an infant from a shipwrecked vessel. The woman could speak no other tongue except the Aboriginal dialects; and when she was placed in an institution in Cooktown she died within four days. Although she refused to eat after her capture she really died of a broken heart, for she kept crying and moaning for the only friends she knew and understood, the Aborigines.

A better-known instance of a white lubra concerns the young Scotswoman Barbara Thompson. Brought to New South Wales by her parents in the late 1830s, she married at the age of sixteen and was with her husband in the cutter *America* when it was driven by a gale onto a reef at Possession Island. Two of the crew were washed overboard and drowned, and on the third day when the storm abated a fleet of canoes manned by natives surrounded the four survivors and killed all except Barbara Thompson, who was taken prisoner.

The story of Barbara Thompson was first known when HMS *Rattlesnake*, an Admiralty survey vessel from Sydney, was in the waters of Torres Strait. Able Seaman Scott with a landing-party from the ship

came ashore at Evans Bay, Cape York. He had orders to obtain birds and animals for scientific purposes, and he brushed aside the natives who clustered round the sailors. The natives gave way as the boat's crew moved across the sands, but a woman stood almost directly in their path. Scott ignored her and walked quickly past, when the woman stumbled forward and cried out in a broken voice, 'I am a white woman! Why do you leave me?'

The startled sailor turned and looked at the woman. She wore only an apron of fibre; she was dirty, her skin was tanned and blistered, one eye was closed, but she was unquestionably a white woman. Scott stared, open-mouthed, bewildered, and when the boat's crew began to crowd round her the woman burst into tears. She was given two of the sailors' shirts, one of which, she wore in the normal style, the other wrapped around her waist as a skirt, and then she was led down to the beach and rowed out to the *Rattlesnake*.

In the captain's cabin the white woman told her story haltingly in a mixture of English and native words. Captain Owen Stanley, RN, half suspecting that she might be an escaped convict from the Moreton Bay penal settlement, asked her gently if she was sure she wanted to be taken back to civilisation. The penalty for runaway convicts was generally death. The young woman, however, assured him that her story was true.

She had lived for about four and a half years mostly on Prince Edward Island, having been taken prisoner on Possession Island. One of the tribal elders, Piaguai, decided that Barbara was the reincarnation of his dead daughter, Giaom. He formally adopted her as his daughter, and she soon found herself a full member of the tribe. From the start her supernatural origin gave her a specially privileged place in the tribe, and she was not expected to work like the other lubras. When the women went out digging yams and carrying heavy loads, she remained in the camps minding the babies. The men treated her with respect, but the women resented this pampered newcomer, although they dared not show their jealousy openly.

Despite privileged treatment Barbara Thompson suffered many hardships. She lost the sight of one eye through contracting an eye disease, and her body was covered with old burn scars through sleeping

124

too close to the fire on cold nights. During her captivity on the island she had occasionally seen ships far out at sea; none had come close enough for her to attract attention. When she learnt by native smoke-signal that a ship was in Evans Bay, she had persuaded three of her tribal 'brothers' to take her to visit the ship in order to obtain axes, knives, and tobacco. The natives had done so, convinced that no one would willingly give up privileged conditions such as she held.

From the day that Barbara boarded the *Rattlesnake* she never left the workroom which Captain Stanley gave her as a cabin. Even when the *Rattlesnake* cruised leisurely about the tropical islands and New Guinea—its whole voyage lasted four years she was too terrified to go ashore. When at length the *Rattlesnake* arrived back in Sydney, Barbara Thompson was able to give authorities much useful information about the natives, including words and grammar of the Muralug, the tribe with whom she lived.

One of the most remarkable stories Mrs Thompson had to tell concerned a mysterious white man who reigned as 'king' on Badu, a nearby island to the one on which she was held captive. She said that, about a year after she had been taken prisoner, her chieftain 'father' received a command from this white man to bring her over to his island of Badu. The chief dared not refuse for fear that his tribe would be wiped out by the native followers of the White Devil.

Strangely enough the white man, a Frenchman, received her with the greatest courtesy. Then he started to boast of his powers, describing how he had trained his savages to kill every white man they saw, to attack every boat that neared his island. The natives carried out his orders to the letter. They were terrified of him and looked upon him as a kind of living devil, which in truth he was. Mrs Thompson said that she was convinced the Frenchman was a madman, and added that, while he was talking to her, he suddenly flew into a violent rage and ordered the chief to take her back. She never saw this extraordinary man again.

On hearing her story, the Queensland Police Department decided to investigate. They sent a small expedition by launch to Badu Island. Sure enough, as they drew near, a fleet of canoes full of armed natives came out to attack them. But the police were ready and, seizing their rifles, picked off the steersman of each canoe. This caused panic among the natives, and they put back to the island. The Frenchman met them on the beach, raging at them in his mad fury and cursing them for their cowardice. He tried to rally them to attack, but it was useless; they fled headlong into the bush. This was too much for their white chief. Seizing a club, he sprang at his own men, killing several before they had time to escape. Very soon he was left alone on the beach.

As the police put in and waded ashore, the Frenchman turned on them. Frothing at the mouth, and with his eyes blazing fearfully, he presented a terrible sight as he rushed toward the new arrivals. He held aloft a spear; his body had been burnt black by the sun and was decorated with necklaces of sharks' teeth. Around his loins was the skin of a shark, and he wore a magnificent head-dress of bird-of-paradise feathers. When the madman halted to hurl his spear at the nearest man, a shot rang out, and without a sound the Frenchman fell dead. So ended the White Devil of Badu.

KING BOONGARIE

The *Sydney Gazette* of 27th November 1830 devoted a good deal of space to the obituary of King Boongarie (or Bungarie), one of the several native chiefs who were 'honoured' with 'badges of distinction' by early governors.

'We have to announce the death of his Aboriginal Majesty King BOONGARIE, Supreme Chief of the Sydney tribe. He expired on Wednesday last, at Garden Island, after a lingering sickness of several months. A coffin has been despatched thither from the Lumber Yard, and he will be interred at Rose Bay beside the remains of his late Queen Gooseberry this day.

'The facetiousness of the sable chief, and the superiority of his mental endowments over those of the generality of his race, obtained for him a more than ordinary share of regard from the white inhabitants of the colony, which was testified by frequent donations suited to his condition, not only from private individuals, but from the Authorities.

'...The late Commodore Sir James Brisbane, was particularly partial to him, and on one occasion presented him with a full suit of his own uniform, together with a sword, of which he was not a little vain. Boongarie had long association with the naval service in various ships of the Royal Navy; and his history was not unknown to the late Commodore. Boongarie accompanied the late Captain Flinders both in the *Norfolk* sloop to Moreton Bay, and in His Majesty's ship *Investigator* to the Gulph of Carpentaria. He also accompanied Commander James Grant in HM Colonial Brig *Lady Nelson* to Port Macquarie. More recently he was with Commander P. P. King in the *Mermaid* cutter on its voyage to the north-west and tropical coasts of Australia.

'For some time past, his increasing infirmities rendered it evident that he could not much longer survive his forefathers; and, on the day above mentioned, in the midst of his own tribe, as well as those of Darling Harbour by all of whom he was greatly beloved, he ended his mortal career. We have not yet heard of his successor; but the honour of course, devolves on the most renowned of his tribe.'

Writing to the *Australian Home Companion* in 1859, a contributor recalled this intriguing personality who had accompanied so many historical maritime expeditions.

'King Boongarie and myself were contemporaries; but there was a vast difference in our ages. When I first knew him he was an old man over sixty, and I was a boy of twelve. Round his neck was suspended, by a brass chain, a brass plate. On this plate, which was shaped like a half moon, were engraved in large letters the words BOONGARRIE, KING OF THE BLACKS. On the plate was also engraved the arms of the colony of New South Wales—an emu and a kangaroo.

'His Majesty changed his manners every five years; or rather they were changed with every administration. Boongarie, like many of the Aborigines of New South Wales, was an amazing mimic. The action, voice, bearing, attitudes, the walk of any man he could personate with astonishing minuteness. It mattered not whether it was the attorney-general stating a case to the jury, the chief-justice sentencing a criminal to be hanged, a colonel drilling a regiment in the barrack square, a Jew bargaining for old clothes, a drunken sailor resisting the efforts of the police to quiet him—King Boongarie could, in mere dumb show, act the scene to give you a perfect idea of it.

'Now as the Governor for the time being was the first and most important person in the colony, it was from that functionary that King Boongarie took his cue. And, after having seen the Governor a few times and talked to him, Boongarie would adopt His Excellency's manner of speech and bearing to the full extent of his wonderful power.

'When first I knew Boongarie, the Governor of New South Wales was General Darling. Boongarie then walked the streets with his arms folded across his breast, his body erect, his pace slow and measured, with something of a military swagger in it, and the only salute he vouchsafed was a dignified but very slight inclination of his head.... But when Darling left and Bourke became his successor how very different was the demeanour and the deportment of King Boongarie! He walked briskly up George Street with his left hand on his hip and his right arm moving to and fro, took off his cocked hat periodically in recognition of salutes (most of them imaginary), and when he neared the guard-house at the bottom of Church Hill he would raise his right hand in the air and shake it, as a signal to the sentry not to turn out the guard to present arms to him.'

SHIPWRECK!

THE FIRST SHIPWRECK

Until but recent times Australia was held to the rest of the world only by ships. Countless vessels have gone to their doom around the Australian coast, or on their journeys to this country, and their tragic stories are of infinite drama. Fire, mutiny, uncharted reefs, heroic open-boat voyages, cannibalism, sturdy ships vanishing without a trace—the Australian sea story is a chronicle that would fill several volumes.

The Monte Bello group of islands off the north-west coast of

Western Australia was the scene of Australia's first recorded shipwreck. Tryal Rocks, the site of the disaster, is named in memory of the vessel. The ill-fated *Tryal* was also the first English ship to sight the then unknown fifth continent. Probably there were many wrecks before the year 1622 on the unnamed Australian coast, but the letters of the *Tryal*'s captain, John Brooke, still preserved in the India Office, London, provide us with this first authentic record.

The *Tryal* left London for Java on an expedition with an eye to East Indies trade. When she ran to her doom on a shelf of rocks on the night of 25th May 1622, she had a company of one hundred and forty-three. Of these, ninety-seven were drowned; the others made a remarkable escape in two small boats. In his letters written from Java nearly three months after the wreck, Captain John Brooke gives a detailed account of the voyage and tells of the disaster with dramatic simplicity.

'Fayre weather and smoothe watter-the shipp strooke ...I ran to the Poope and hove the leads. I found but three fadom watter, 60 men being upon deck, five of them would not believe that she had strooke, I cryings to them to beare up and tacke to westward.

'They did ther beste, but the rocke being sharpe the shipp was presentlie full of watter. For the most part these rocks lie two fadom under watter. It struck my men in such a mayze when I said the shipp strooke and they could see neyther breach, land, rocks, change of watter nor signe of danger...the hold of the shipp was full of watter in an instant.'

When he saw there was no hope of saving the ship, the captain got out the long-boat and hung her in the tackles over the side. The most it could hold was thirty-six, and these he put under the supervision of Thomas Bright who immediately put off from the stricken vessel and headed in the general direction of Java '...128 soules were left to God's mercye' on the wreck.

Within a day or two the fore part of the *Tryal* tore way from the hull and crashed into the sea. The remainder of the ship could not last much longer, and the sweeping seas were already marked by the flashing fins of sharks. Hunger and thirst would soon begin to prey upon the men as they waited, helplessly, for the coming of death. Then it was that Captain John Brooke, the only one left capable of navigation, decided also to make an attempt to reach Java in a small skiff. And so, with nine companions, he set off.

The provisions in the little skiff consisted of forty pounds of bread and one barrel of water, but the latter was conserved because for four days there was continuous rain. They reached a small island but it was completely barren, so they lost no time there and kept on their course. On the fifteenth day, to their joy, they sighted the east end of the island of Java and, continuing their journey, reached Batavia after another sixteen days.

Thomas Bright and the thirty-five men in the long-boat also arrived safely. But no rescue vessels put back into the uncharted sea on the off chance of finding the unknown rocks and the wreckage. Had they done so, they would have been too late to succour those left on the *Tryal*; by the time the survivors reached Java every one of the ninety-seven men left behind must have gone to his sailor's grave, and it was useless sending living men after dead ones.

A MARINE GRAVEYARD

Not without cause was King Island given the ominous title 'the marine graveyard of Bass Strait'. What tragedies were enacted on that 120 miles of inhospitable coastline before the discovery of the island nobody will ever know, but a list of all recorded wrecks there places the total number of ships lost at sixty, with a death-roll of over two thousand lives.

There was one wreck from which a cat was the sole survivor. With what ship the cat sailed has never become known, but the nameless vessel from which it escaped represents the first recorded shipwreck on the island. On 18th March 1802 a sealer named Campbell in his small ship *Harrington* dropped anchor off this island, which was not shown on his chart. He went ashore looking for fresh water for the *Harrington*'s depleted tanks, and along the beach where he landed he saw scattered portions of a ship's wreckage. There was nothing to indicate the name of the vessel, or its country, only the 'cat Crusoe'. Unknown to Campbell, the island had been officially marked on the map one year before by Captain John Black in the *Harbinger* and named after Governor King of New South Wales.

One of the island's earliest recorded disasters was the wreck of the *Neva*, which went ashore in 1835. When she left Cork, Ireland, the *Neva* carried 240 people including 150 women convicts, 9 free women and 55 children. After the *Neva* struck the reefs off King Island during a furious storm in Bass Strait, only 22 souls reached the shore and 7 of these died before rescue reached them.

The following extracts are from a Launceston newspaper of July 1835, telling of the disaster:

'. . . At five a.m. a reef was reported to be seen right ahead. The ship came head to wind, and while in stays, struck. The rudder was carried away, the wheel fell on deck, and the vessel being unmanageable paved off before the wind. In a few minutes she took a reef on her larboard bow, and struck violently. A sea hove her broadside on, and bilged her—the next that followed made a fair breach over her, and swept many of the unfortunate women overboard.

'The pinnace was hove out, and the Captain, Surgeon, and several women got in, but before she could be shoved from the wreck, so many women rushed into her that she sank alongside. The Captain and two others recovered the wreck. The long-boat was then launched, into which most of the crew and several women consigned themselves, but she had scarcely cleared the wreck when a sea capsized her, and the whole number, excepting the Captain and the Chief Mate, met a watery grave. These two a second time recovered the vessel.

'The *Neva* soon after separated into four parts, the deck leaving her top, and dividing formed two rafts. The scene now became the most heart-rending that ever was witnessed by human eyes. The number of females, some holding children up, and at the same time drowning themselves, was so dreadful that the survivors turned away from the sight with horror. On one of the rafts the Captain and several of the surviving women held fast; the first officer, with some others, clung to the other. They floated clear of the wreck, and the hapless people, after clinging to them for eight hours drifted into a sandy bay. The raft upon which was the first officer, being disengaged from the rigging and gear, went well inshore, and most of the people were saved from it. Those upon the Captain's raft were not so fortunate—a large portion of the vessel's foremast stuck through it, and occasioned it to ground when about half a mile off-shore. A tremendous surf rolled upon the beach, which broke upon the raft, and swept from it every individual. The Captain, a seaman and a woman gained the shore, the rest of this ill-fated little band perished in the surf.

'Twenty-two persons all told reached the shore alive—seven of whom died during the next day, either from over-exertion, or injuries received in the melancholy struggle for life. Out of the *Neva's* complement of 240, fifteen only have been saved. These poor people made the best of their distressing situation upon King Island. They built for themselves a tent out of a topmast, studding sail, and gaff topsail, washed on shore, and supported themselves upon shellfish which they procured from the rocks, and from the fragments of provisions that were occasionally cast up...'

The newspaper then records how, by an extraordinary coincidence, some survivors from another shipwreck, the *Tartar*, which went to pieces on the south-east end of the island some weeks previously, were attracted by the wreckage floating about. They undertook a search around the island and fell in with the *Neva* survivors. They were able to help them with food—wallabies which they had caught—and the combined survivors kept together until their rescue the following month.

THE *CATARAQUI*

The *Cataraqui* was an emigrant ship with 423 people aboard*, and of this number only 9 survived the voyage. The tragedy occurred at night and was a scene of unparalleled horror—the greatest number of people to die at one time on the King Island coast, and one of the heaviest losses of life in the whole history of Australian shipping disasters. The ship was 106 days out from Liverpool, with English emigrants for Melbourne, when she crashed into a reef on the western side of the island on 4th August 1845. The *Port Phillip Herald* of 13th September 1845 contained the first account of the catastrophe:

'It is our melancholy duty to lay before the public the particulars of

The Australian Encyclopaedia gives the number of people on board the *Cataraqui* as 415.

the most awful shipwreck which has ever occurred in these colonies—
the total wreck of the emigrant ship *Cataraqui*, upon the iron bound
coast of King Island...

'The following particulars are from Mr Guthrie, the chief mate,
who, with his eight fellow survivors, reached the shore almost in a state
of nudity, having of course lost everything they possessed...

'Immediately the ship struck, she was sounded, four feet of water
being in her hold. The scene of confusion and misery that ensued at
this awful period, it is impossible to describe. All the passengers
attempted to rush on deck, and many succeeded in doing so, until the
ladders were knocked away by the workings of the vessel; when the
shrieks from men, women, and children from below were terrific,
calling on the watch on deck to assist them.

'The crew to a man were on deck the moment the ship struck, and
were instantly employed in handing up passengers. Up to the time the
vessel began breaking up it is supposed that between three and four
hundred were got on deck by the extraordinary exertions of the crew.
At this time the sea was breaking over the ship on the larboard side,
sweeping the decks, every sea taking away passengers.

'At five a.m., the ship careened right over on her larboard side,
washing away boats, bulwarks, spars, a part of the cuddy, and literally
swept the decks. At this critical period the captain gave orders to cut
away the masts, hoping the vessel might right itself to enable the crew
to get on deck the passengers left below. The masts were forthwith cut
away and everything done that could, under the circumstances, to get
the vessel upright, but it was all to no purpose.

'At this time the passengers below were all drowned, the ship being
full of water, and the captain called out to those on deck to cling to that
part of the wreck which was then above water, till day-light, hoping
that the spars would be of some service in making a breakwater under
her lee, and thus enable the survivors to get on shore in the morning.

'As the day broke we found the stem of the vessel washed in, and
numerous dead bodies floating round the ship—some hanging upon
the rocks. About two hundred passengers and crew were still holding
on to the vessel—the sea breaking over and every wave washing some
of them away. Those who were able continued to cling to the wreck

until about four in the afternoon, when she parted amidships, at the fore part of the main rigging. Immediately about one hundred were hurled into the remorseless seas…The remains of the upper deck now began to break up and wash away.

'The survivors began to collect bits of rope, so as to construct a buoy, with the view of floating it on shore, and thus enabling one of the crew to land. This measure would have enabled them to save the lives of at least a hundred. But, notwithstanding every effort, the buoy could not be got nearer than twenty yards from the shore, owing to its getting entangled with the sea-weed on the rocks, and there was no one on shore to catch it and secure it on the beach.

'The fury of the waves continuing unabated, about five o'clock the wreck parted by the fore rigging, and so many souls were submerged in the tumultuous waters that only seventy survivors were left crowded on the forecastle. The buoy rope was then hauled on board to rig life lines and lash the survivors, who were then clinging to the wreck. Thus the sea breaking over them, the winds raging, and the rain continuing heavy all night, the poor survivors remained clinging to the vessel's bow. Many died and fell overboard or sank and were drowned at the places where they were lashed.

'As the day broke the following morning it discovered only about 30 left alive—the survivors nearly dead through exhaustion and hanging where they were lashed. The sea was making a clean breech into the forecastle, the deck of which was rapidly breaking up.

'The lashings of the survivors were now undone to give them the last chance of life. Mr Thomas Guthrie, the chief mate, seized a piece of plank under his arm and leaping into the water was carried over the reef, and thus got on shore. He found a passenger who had got ashore during the night, and one of the crew who got ashore in the morning. John Roberts, a seaman, plunged in when he saw the mate ashore, and partly swimming and partly driven reached the land. Five other seamen followed, and got ashore dreadfully exhausted. Almost immediately afterwards the vessel totally disappeared. Thus out of four hundred and twenty-three souls on board, only nine were saved. The names of the saved are…

'The survivors had neither food nor drink from the time of the ship

135

striking to Tuesday afternoon, when they found one small tin of preserved fowl, after eating which, they went and laid down in the bush, having got a wet blanket out of the water for their only covering and being almost destitute of clothes. The beach was strewed with pieces of wreckage and portions of dead bodies in ghastly profusion. After a vain search for water, and being unable to find any more survivors, they slept that night in the bush....'

The *Port Phillip Herald* then recounts how David Howie and three other sealers found the survivors who were taken to Melbourne on the schooner *Midge*. Howie, who received a medal for his rescue of the survivors, found 314 bodies and buried them in five graves.

The survivors reported that when nearing King Island the *Cataraqui* had met heavy weather, which had made observations impossible. Before the ship struck, Captain Finlay wished to heave to, but yielded to the insistence of Edward Carpenter, the senior of his two surgeons, who demanded that he continue on to Port Phillip. Ironical is the fact that Solomon Brown, the only surviving emigrant (his wife and children were lost), was drowned three years later in water only eighteen inches deep, in a creek near Port Phillip. Another of the nine survivors, the first mate, Thomas Guthrie, was in command of the *Tigress* when she was wrecked near Adelaide just a year after the *Cataraqui* disaster. Only one life was lost—Thomas Guthrie.

D'Entrecasteaux Channel Shipwrecks

The grotesquely shaped indentation on the south-eastern coastline of Tasmania known as D'Entrecasteaux Channel has witnessed many a sea tragedy since it was first charted by the French admiral, Bruni d'Entrecasteaux. Two of its major disasters occurred within two months of each other, the wrecks of the *George III* and the *Enchantress* in 1835.

The first was the convict ship *George III*, carrying 208 male prisoners from England to the penal settlement at Port Arthur. The vessel was literally within sight of its destination when it entered the channel and ran aground on the rocks. As it commenced to settle down, the captain and his officers saw that the position was not desperate as regards getting off the vessel and rowing over to Bruny Island, but the military guards were frightened that the convicts might panic and break out of the hold. To forestall such a contingency they fired muskets indiscriminately amongst the prisoners to intimidate them into acceptance of their fate. This could hardly be expected to calm their fears. To quote an eyewitness: 'There being some panic among the unfortunate beings below-deck, and some attempt on their part to preserve their lives or to commit themselves to the mercy of the water, shots were fired among them to deter them from this course, and they were given the choice of dying by drowning or by musket fire.' The total convict death-roll in that dreadful happening was 120, but of the deaths from shooting and those from drowning the numbers are not stated. Of the 134 lives lost on the *George III*, 13 were crew members and sergeants' wives and children.

The second sea tragedy in the channel, just two months later, also occurred on treacherous rocks. Under the command of Captain Roxborough, the *Enchantress* was bringing a company of some fifty free settlers to Van Diemen's Land (as Tasmania was then known), when she piled up there and her bowsprit was carried away. There were but three survivors: three men who got safely away in the only seaworthy ship's boat. The fortunate trio comprised the captain, the chief officer, and the ship's surgeon. As one chronicler has stated, these three, according to the strictest traditions of the sea, should definitely not have been the saved ones, and it seems that the 'every man for himself' principle was employed.

THE *DUNBAR* DISASTER

Not much happens at Watson's Bay nowadays, and even those distressing occasions when some poor soul decides to go over the Gap have lost much of their news value because of their frequency.

Yet in the 1850s Watson's Bay was a really important place, and its postmaster was an important man in the life of the colony. When a ship was sighted off the coast the signal master told the postmaster, and the postmaster sent word through to Sydney, and the merchants of Sydney Town began to get ready to receive the cargo that would arrive in due course, if the wind held fair.

There was not much business transacted in Watson's Bay Post

THE *DUNBAR*

Office on 20th August 1857; it was just a day in spring with nothing to suggest the tragedy the following dawn was to bring.

But in the black of that night, approaching the entrance to Port Jackson, the sailing-ship *Dunbar* was to be dashed to pieces on the rocks below the cliffs between the Gap and the lighthouse. All except one of the ship's total company of 122 were drowned.

Ill news travels fast. On that tragedy-laden day of 1857 all Sydney came from near and far to Watson's Bay. Clerk, merchant and artisan, over the sandhills and out along the South Head Road, by buggy and coach or on foot, the rich and poor—social barriers for the moment forgotten—searching each crevice and scanning each wave for what it might return from the sea. On the second morning the curious crowds on the clifftops saw the sole survivor of the ghastly wreck, Seaman Johnson. He was clinging half-way up the cliffs on a ledge where the waves had left him, and where he had spent more than thirty-six hours. They hauled him up with ropes.

During succeeding days bodies were dashed by heavy seas, the spray from which came over the top of the cliffs. Wreckage of all description and mutilated bodies were found on the beaches of North and Middle harbours. At the inquest Johnson was the only person who could give an eyewitness account of the *Dunbar* disaster.

'All that day,' he said 'the ship's rails were lined by English emigrants trying to catch a glimpse of the coast. They didn't seem to mind the south-easterly gale that was blowing. Just before dusk they sighted the dim outline of Botany Bay, six miles off. Then a heavy rain-squall developed as darkness fell.

'Late that night the *Dunbar* battled her way up to Port Jackson, fighting all the time to stand safely off the shore. Through the rain an occasional flash came from the South Head lighthouse. I heard Captain Green shouting to the mate, "Do you see anything of North Head?" The mate called back that he could see nothing.

'Then through the lashing storm I heard a faint cry from the second mate on the fo'c'sle head, "Breakers ahead!" Captain Green called to the steerman to put the helm hard aport, and to the crew to "Haul in the port braces and brace the yards up sharp!"

'The ship shuddered. The next instant, before she could grip onto changed course, the *Dunbar* took a crashing broadside leap onto the rocks. Bulwarks and lifeboats went skipping away in great jagged pieces. Masts snapped with a crack that could be heard above the storm. The waves picked up human beings as well as wreckage, tossed them onto the surf and battered them against the rocks.

'In the few minutes the *Dunbar* lasted, a steward, at Captain Green's order, lit a signal fire, but the feeble blue light was useless. The next minute the hull itself began to break up. It was all over. No amount of signalling or seamanship could save the *Dunbar* or anyone on her.'

Of the 121 people killed or drowned, only 31 bodies were ever found, some of them being washed up on beaches after the mass burial in the old Camperdown Cemetery. The remains of one person were buried in the vicinity of Manly Beach. The procession of mourners at the mass funeral left the morgue at five o'clock in the afternoon, but with nearly all of Sydney's population thronging the streets the cortege was delayed and it was dark when they reached the cemetery. The service was conducted by lamplight.

At the conclusion of the inquest on the *Dunbar* the jury recorded a

verdict that 'there may have been an error in judgment in the vessel being so close to the shore at night in such bad weather, but they do not attach any blame to Captain Green or his officers for the loss of the *Dunbar*'. The masters of thirty-five ships in Port Jackson at the time of the inquest made a joint statement to the effect that the captain's action in bearing up for the port was a judicious one, and had they been placed in similar circumstances they should have considered it their duty to run for the harbour.

Despite the widespread belief that the *Dunbar*'s captain made the mistake of confusing the Gap with the entrance to the harbour, the loss of the vessel was apparently due to the rapid leeway she made between Botany Bay and Sydney Heads.

For years afterwards many old people expressed the passage of time by referring to so many years before or after 'the wreck of the *Dunbar*'. James Johnson was afterwards employed at Newcastle lighthouse and while there helped to rescue the only survivor of the wreck of the ship *Cawarra* in 1866. The anchor of the *Dunbar* was recovered more than half a century later and placed on the cliffs at Watson's Bay; a memorial tablet is placed alongside. In recent years amateur skindivers of Sydney located the wreck and recovered various relics from it. Many other relics of the *Dunbar*, which were picked up on Sydney Harbour beaches at the time of the tragedy, are still preserved.

There are tombstones in South Head Cemetery to remind the visitor of the shipwreck, and in St James' Church, Sydney, is a tablet to the memory of Captain James Green. But the monument to Johnson will be found in one of the back streets of Paddington—the old Dunbar Hotel, purchased for him by a sympathetic public.

The *Charles Eaton* Massacre

In mid-August 1834 a raft grounded ashore on Aureed Island, off Cape York. Six men, two women and two children, survivors from the wreck of the barque *Charles Eaton*, trudged wearily ashore. Suddenly a mob of shrieking natives fell on the tragic party. The eight adults were butchered and their heads hacked off as gruesome trophies; despite this barbaric slaughter neither of the children, George D'Oyley (aged seven) and his brother William (aged two), had a finger laid on them by the bloodthirsty natives. A few days later ship's boy John Ireland and cabin-boy John Sexton, who had survived the same wreck, were brought to the island where they were held in close captivity with the other children for two months.

At the end of this period the natives separated into two parties and left the island. John Sexton and George D'Oyley went with one group and were never heard of again. John Ireland and William D'Oyley, in one of the most remarkable island episodes in Australian history, lived for two years with a tribe of cannibals and head-hunters notorious throughout Cape York Peninsula and the Torres Strait for their savagery.

The *Charles Eaton*, a barque of 313 tons, had sailed from Sydney on a voyage to Surabaya and Canton with a crew of twenty-three under the command of Captain Frederick Moore. Her passengers were Dr Grant, George Armstrong (a London barrister), and Captain D'Oyley of the East India Company's Artillery who was accompanied by his wife, two sons, and an Indian servant woman.

When the vessel was well out to sea off Cape Grenville, a heavy storm threatened to rip her canvas to shreds. Captain Moore decided to sail through a narrow channel in the Great Barrier Reef to calmer water. As the ship churned ahead at great speed, the man on the lookout suddenly shouted a warning. Breakers lay dead ahead. The *Charles Eaton* altered course, but, before she could gather way on the new tack, a huge sea caught her broadside and smashed her on a jagged reef off Sir Charles Hardy Island. That submerged reef afterwards was marked Detached Reef on shipping charts. The ship was held fast, and there was no immediate danger unless the weather worsened. Unluckily the gale increased in force and, when the captain ordered the longboat to be launched to investigate how much buffeting the hulk would stand, a giant wave smashed it to splinters against the coral. During a momentary calm a smaller cutter was launched, manned by seaman James Price. Tragedy struck again when another hissing green mountain of water bore down crushing man and boat in the coral-studded sea; neither was seen again.

Only one boat, a cutter capable of holding no more than eight persons, remained. George Piggott, the bosun, Laurence Constantine, a carpenter, and a seaman quickly lowered it and the three of them pushed clear of the wreck. As it began to move away, two other seamen leapt from the slowly disintegrating hull, swam to the boat and were dragged aboard. Then the five deserters pulled away, leaving passengers and the rest of the crew marooned on the doomed barque.

All through that night those on the wreck suffered agonies of mind wondering whether they would live to see the next day, but dawn broke on a clear sky and calm waters. With a measure of hope the men began to build a raft from loose timbers on the vessel. When finished, and the sun shining, the raft was launched and found to float well. Mrs D'Oyley and her two boys together with the Bengalese woman servant were first placed on it, followed by some of the men. A second raft was found necessary to hold the rest of the ship's company, and while this was being built the first one paddled off.

After a perilous voyage this first raft finally grounded to rest on Aureed Island, where the survivors were attacked by the head-hunters and only the lives of two-year-old William D'Oyley and his seven-year-old brother, George, were spared. The second raft drifted for seven days, the castaways existing on a daily ration of two draughts of water and half a ship's biscuit. When they reached the island of Boydong, about forty miles north-west of the wreck, they, too, were attacked by natives and all were massacred except the two boys, John Ireland and John Sexton. It was not long before the boys were taken by canoe to Aureed Island where they joined the two other young survivors.

The natives on Aureed came from different islands. After a lot of haggling among the chiefs, when the time came for their return to their islands the four boy prisoners were divided. One party took George D'Oyley and John Sexton, never to be heard of or seen again, while John Ireland and William D'Oyley were taken to Marsden Island where they were well treated and kept as curiosities. Natives from all parts of the Torres Strait visited Marsden Island to look at the strange white children who had come out of the sea. It was believed that they were reincarnations of deceased natives.

Among the visitors was a chief named Duppah, who also brought his wife with him. They took such a fancy to the boys that the chief bought them for two bunches of bananas. Duppah then carried off his prizes to his home on Mer, now called Murray Island. One day the trading vessel *Mangles*, under the command of Captain William Carr, anchored off Mer Island. Among the natives who came out in canoes to trade was John Ireland. He told the captain the tragic story of the wreck of the *Charles Eaton*, but when he was offered a chance to escape he was reluctant, saying that he was happy enough and contented. Next day Captain Carr landed on the island to investigate the story and, sure enough, saw the young boy William D'Oyley, whom the natives made no attempt to hide.

When Captain Carr eventually returned to Sydney and revealed the news of the two young castaways on Mer Island, Governor Bourke took action. As a result the colonial cutter *Isabella*, under the command of Captain Lewis, left Sydney for Torres Strait in May 1836. It was nearly two years after the wreck that the *Isabella* reached Mer Island. This time John Ireland decided to return to civilisation, and the chief, Duppah, did not mind parting with him. Duppah boarded the *Isabella*, quite ready to trade the white youth for a bright new hatchet. He was unwilling, however, to hand over William D'Oyley, who had become a great favourite of his wife and himself and, indeed, the pet of all the islanders. Eventually, but with great reluctance, Duppah agreed to surrender the boy in exchange for another tomahawk, but young Will D'Oyley cried bitterly when taken from his native foster mother. When he was rescued the boy had no knowledge of English, but he could speak the native island language fluently for a child of four.

Captain Lewis' task was also to get proof of the wreck and to account as far as possible for all the ship's company. On leaving Murray (Mer) Island with the two young survivors, he visited Aureed Island. Ireland's memory of the tragic events enabled Lewis to find a hideous memento of the slaughter on Aureed Island. It was a huge turtle-shell painted to resemble a mask, and around the edge of it were a number of skulls tied with rope of European origin. The skulls were identified as those of white people, with the hair still attached. Judging from the long locks of one, it was the skull of a woman, and the comb which was still in the hair suggested strongly that it was all that remained of Mrs D'Oyley. The skulls were brought back to Sydney and were finally buried in the cemetery at Bunnerong. Today, a headstone over the grave records that under it are interred the skulls brought back from the Torres Strait island by Captain Lewis of the *Isabella*. The comb which adorned the hair of the female skull is—at least, it was until recent years—in the possession of a Queenslander.

Governor Bourke rewarded Captain Lewis for his part in the rescue by appointing him harbour-master at Port Phillip, Victoria. Young Will D'Oyley was taken into the household of a Mrs Anne Slade in Sydney, but later Lewis took the youngster to England and placed him in the care of his father's family. There he grew up to follow his father's profession in the service of the East India Company. John Ireland settled down to a job ashore and never returned to the sea.

As to the five deserters from the wreck of the *Charles Eaton*, they sailed through Torres Strait, and one man died before the rest reached Timor-Laut. From there they made their way to Amboina where they told their story, colouring it to justify their desertion. In due course a trading vessel took them to England, where they were able to add further information on the loss of the *Charles Eaton*.

Wreck of the *Quetta*

One of Australia's worst coastal shipping disasters was the wreck of the *Quetta*. A fine, trim ship, she was one of the latest passenger steamers on the London-Brisbane run and was regarded as safe and seaworthy as any to be found on the seven seas. When she departed from the Brisbane wharf in February 1890, her passengers had a gay send-off from friends which was slightly marred by the ship's stem grazing a shed on the edge of the wharf, tearing off yards of planking with a splintering crash. However, she soon righted herself with the drag of the tug's hawsers and, without further incident, steamed off. Nevertheless, superstitious members of the crew regarded the bad start as an ominous sign.

It was a smooth and uneventful voyage all along the North Australian coast until the evening of 28th February 1890, when the *Quetta* was travelling through Adolphus Channel in Torres Strait at 13 knots. It was a night of radiant moonlight with the sea exceptionally calm, and many of the passengers were strolling along the decks admiring the beauty of the tropical seascape. Captain Saunders was on the bridge with the pilot, who was taking the ship through the channel. He knew every rock and shoal, and there was little need for him to consult the Admiralty charts, so carefully plotted over years of oceanic survey.

A few minutes after the ship's bell rang 9, the *Quetta* struck something with a grinding crash that made the vessel shudder from stem to stem. She floundered off course as the engines stopped. It was thought that the *Quetta* had collided with a derelict, but seconds later the stunned captain realised that the impossible had happened; the vessel had struck an uncharted rock.

He shouted to the chief officer to launch the boats as the *Quetta* heeled over to port at a sickening angle. Water was pouring into the ship through the huge rent the rock had sheared in her side, trapping the engine-room crew and firemen. Bewildered and frantic passengers clung to the rails as Captain Saunders strove with his officers to get the women and children first into the boats. But the panic-stricken Lascar crew and some Javanese passengers frustrated their efforts, and in a frenzy of fear rushed the boats trampling down and thrusting aside all who opposed them.

The British officers fought them with their fists and drew their revolvers, but the Lascars managed to get away in the first two boats, one of which was swamped with its weight of numbers, and the occupants flung into the water. Most of the women and children were able to be accommodated in the remaining boats before the *Quetta* took her final plunge.

There were many tragic happenings on that dreadful night, and of the 982 people aboard the *Quetta* only 109 were saved. The heavy loss of life was primarily due to the fact that the coloured crew became unmanageable. Surviving passengers described how screaming Lascars had seized them in the water and scrambled into one of the boats with women and children until their numbers caused it to overturn.

The mystery of the uncharted rock was later solved, when survey vessels found that it was a pinnacle of growing coral which had built up over the thirty-odd years since the earlier surveys had been made.

One of the three female survivors of the wreck, Mrs Alice Horsley, died in Brisbane in November 1951 at the age of eighty-one. Another was the late Mrs Cecil McDonald, of Southport, Queensland. She was a baby when the *Quetta* went to her doom. Nurse Fitzgerald, of Thursday Island, played an important part in the rescue of the baby. In those days it was the custom of the authorities, for obvious reasons, to fire bullets into the bodies which rose to the surface after several days, and Nurse Fitzgerald was on the beach while operations were being carried out. What looked like a dead body appeared on the water and the police officer had raised his rifle when the nurse, thinking she saw some signs of life in the victim, stopped the officer from firing.

A boat was rowed out and a girl, burnt quite black and completely nude, was lifted into it and brought to land, where Nurse Fitzgerald nursed her back to health. None of the *Quetta* survivors could identify the child, and Captain Brown, the Torres Strait pilot, adopted her and she grew up under the name of Quetta Brown. She afterwards married a relative of the captain.

THE SINKING OF THE *AUSTRAL*

In November 1882 the Orient liner *Austral* entered Sydney Harbour on her maiden voyage. Surpassed in size only by the *Great Eastern* the *Austral* was a screw vessel with beautiful lines and elaborately fitted for passenger service. The second largest steamer in the world, and the finest ship that had ever come to Australia, she was an object of intense interest to all the citizens of Sydney. After the passengers had disembarked and the cargo had been discharged, the vessel was towed to Neutral Bay to take in coal—the usual procedure.

The following morning ferry passengers on passing Neutral Bay stared with amazement when they saw only the upper structure and masts of the *Austral* visible above the water. The pride of the Orient Company had foundered while taking coal, because somebody had neglected to close her lower ports. Four of the crew were drowned.

The tragedy happened in the early hours of the morning while most of the officers and crew were asleep in their berths. So quickly did the *Austral* sink that, in a matter of minutes, she was resting on the harbour bottom. The ship had been coaling the previous day and all through the night. The method followed was the usual one: the port and starboard bunkers were filled separately.

As the coal poured in, the ship commenced to list slightly. No attention was paid to this because, even with full bunkers on one side only, there was normally no danger of a capsize. Just as the work of filling the bunkers on the opposite side was about to commence, the men were alarmed to discover that water was pouring into the vessel through the lower ports; somebody had forgotten to close them before coaling commenced. Hundreds of tons of water were flowing in every minute, and no human power could close the ports against the inrush.

The raising of such a large vessel presented a tremendous problem, but it was solved. Divers descended, and after closing the ports made all apertures watertight. A great wooden dam was built up from the harbour bottom. The walls of this basin were made in sections and lowered to the divers, who clamped and fastened them into position. When all was ready, the great pumps began to suck the water from the hull. But so great was the external pressure that the caulking of the wooden planks began to leak.

The salvage engineers then decided to encase the whole dam with canvas. It took thousands of square feet of canvas, but proved successful. At the end of February, 1883, four months after the fatality, the pumps were again set to work and this time the few leaks were controllable by the divers. Two days later the *Austral* began slowly to rise to the surface. When the shipwrights had completed their work, she came out of dock as fine a vessel as before, but someone's carelessness in not closing the ports had cost four men their lives and the Orient Company a fortune.

THE *MIGNONETTE* TRAGEDY

A former New South Wales Attorney-General was a keen yachting enthusiast. In 1884 he purchased a luxury yacht in England named the *Mignonette*, and engaged a captain and crew to sail the craft from Southampton to Sydney. On the voyage out the vessel ran into a violent storm, and on 5th July foundered when 1600 miles from Cape Agulhas, South Africa.

The *Mignonette* sank so fast that the crew had only five minutes to take to the long-boat. While the giant waves buffeted the yacht, Captain Dudley's crew of three—the mate Edwin Stevens, deck-hand Edward Brooks and the 17-year-old ship's boy, Richard Parker—clambered into the boat. The skipper quickly followed them, hastily grabbing two tins of food as he did so. There was no water aboard the long-boat and, to add to the men's plight, the two tins of food turned out to contain turnips instead of meat. For the next nineteen days they doled out the scanty supply of turnips until there was nothing left; they managed to catch a turtle floating on the surface and this helped to sustain them for a while. The castaways took off their shirts and pieced them together to make a rough sail, which helped their progress, but they were so far off the main shipping route that there was little chance of being picked up.

With the last of the foodstuff gone, their position was desperate in the extreme. Meanwhile Parker had been drinking sea water and was in the last stages of exhaustion. He was lying in the bottom of the boat, when Dudley and the mate decided to kill him for food. The captain, asking God to forgive him, said, 'Richard, my boy, your time has come.' He then stuck his pocket-knife in Parker's neck, killing him instantly. Although deck-hand Brooks disapproved of the killing, holding that they should live or die together, he ate his share of the boy's flesh.

Four days later, after spending a total of twenty-four days in the open boat and drifting 1,000 miles with the currents, the three survivors were picked up by the German vessel *Montezuma* and landed at Falmouth. There Captain Dudley reported the tragedy to the Collector of Customs, making a clean breast of the killing of the youth. The three men were taken to the Falmouth Police Court where they were charged with murder on the high seas. However, when the case was heard at the Exeter Assizes, only Dudley and Stevens were put on trial.

The jury could not reach a verdict; they reported they were unable to do so because of the extraordinary circumstances. They were of the opinion that had not the three fed on the body of the youth they would probably not have survived, and that he, in any case, was likely to have died before them. Moreover, as the survivors claimed, they had to consider their wives and families who were dependent on them. And so the case was referred to the Court of Queen's Bench in London.

Here after hearing counsel's arguments, England's Lord Chief Justice delivered judgment on 9th December 1884. The real question, he said, was whether killing in such circumstances was or was not murder. He and his fellow judges believed that it was wilful murder and that the facts furnished no legal justification of homicide. No matter how awful the suffering, how terrible the temptation, there was no excuse for murder. The taking of life for the safeguarding of one's own could only be justified in self defence against physical violence. Though preserving one's life was a duty, it must never be done at the expense of the life of another. War, said the Lord Chief Justice, showed countless instances of a man's duty not to live, but to die.

However, in delivering the judgment of guilty, the Lord Chief Justice did not assume the black cap. Sentence of death was passed with a recommendation to the clemency of the Crown, and the two men were taken back to prison where they served six months before being reprieved.

The case naturally created a sensation in Australia, and a ballad was composed on the subject which soon became a favourite song. Here is one verse:

> On the Atlantic Ocean
> Starving night and day
> Death will be your Portion
> Unless the boy you slay.
>
> Amid the waves and billows
> His life they did destroy
> And now in Heaven dwells the soul
> Of Dick the cabin-boy.

THE MAP WAS WRONG
The wreck of the *Elingamite* was made more tragic by the unbelievable fact that it was caused through a wrongly marked map. Yet the vessel's doom possibly averted other disasters and resulted in the formation of the National Shipwreck Relief Society of New Zealand.

On the fatal voyage in November 1902 the *Elingamite*, a steel screw steamer of the Huddart Parker Interstate Service, sailed from Sydney under the command of Captain Attwood. The ship had a smooth and uneventful passage on its voyage to Auckland until the fourth day out of port, when an early-morning fog gathered round her. The grey blanket thickened, and with the captain and third officer on the bridge and lookouts posted the fog siren was sounded at close intervals.

Without any indication of danger the ship gave a fearful shudder as she crashed suddenly on a rock that tore a great jagged hole in her hull. Water poured into the *Elingamite* as she quickly began to sink to her

deck level, but there were no signs of panic on the doomed vessel. Captain Attwood saw to it that the boats and life rafts were launched and filled with passengers and crew in a quiet and speedy manner. 'I could not say enough of Captain Attwood's pluck,' said one of the survivors. 'No words could describe his bravery. He was the last to leave the wreck, being washed overboard. He stood on two pieces of wreckage, one foot on each, as they rocked about in the open sea, and there he blew his whistle, the sound which brought up a boat.'

Giving evidence at the marine inquiry, one of the passengers told of her experience in the open sea.

'I was on a raft with fifteen others. It was too great a load, and our plight was made more difficult because the air cylinders of the raft were more than half awash and the decking was actually under water. We were never dry. Between the sixteen of us, all we had were two apples and no drinking water whatsoever. Still, we cheered each other with the thought that help would quickly be sent. But when the second day passed, our hunger and thirst made us feel almost hopeless.

'All this time we were drifting aimlessly out of sight of land and ships. The sea washed constantly over the raft, and our throats swelled with thirst. By the third day four of our number were dead. That night we saw a ship. It came close and we mustered all our strength and shouted repeatedly. Again and again we shouted but it was all in vain; the ship disappeared from our sight. It was too much for one of the passengers—he became delirious and jumped overboard. [It transpired that the vessel which had come within a few miles of the raft without seeing it was the *Omapere*, sent by the Union Steamship Company to search for survivors.]

'When daylight came we cut up the remaining apple which had been kept as long as possible. We divided it into eleven pieces, and ate one piece each. That day another man jumped overboard, and a stewardess died. Four hours later the rescue ship *Penguin* saw our raft. We were so exhausted that it was thought when we were sighted through the ship's telescope that we were all dead on the raft.'

When the government survey ship *Penguin* rescued the survivors, it was ascertained that the raft had floated about sixty-six miles north by east from the scene of the wreck. Thirty lives were lost in the wreck.

High tribute was paid to Captain Attwood's efficiency and conduct at the critical time of the disaster, but the official inquiry found that since the *Elingamite* was wrecked on the islands known as the Three Kings, this was proof that the vessel was off course. Not only was the captain's certificate suspended, but he was ordered to pay part of the cost of the inquiry.

Ruined by the finding and unable to accept command of another ship, Captain Attwood's life for the next four years was an unhappy one, and his health suffered accordingly. Then, in 1906, the vessel *Elberland* went to her doom on the same rocks off the Three Kings. At the same time the extraordinary discovery was made that the Three Kings' position was wrongly marked on the Admiralty charts. Captain Attwood's loss, like that of the captain of the *Elberland*, had not been due to bad seamanship but to wrongly marked maps. Captain Attwood's certificate was restored to him immediately, and he was paid compensation from the Government, but he died shortly after he learnt that the tragedy of the *Elingamite* was not his fault.

THE *STIRLING CASTLE*

The wreck of the *Stirling Castle* and its outcome is a sorry tale, a story of a woman's amazing fortitude and the miserable death of a gallant band of British seamen. On 15th May 1836 the brig *Stirling Castle* sailed from Sydney on a voyage to Singapore via North Queensland. In addition to his crew, Captain James Fraser had his wife, Eliza, a native of Stromness in the Orkneys, on board together with his thirteen-year-old nephew. One week out from Sydney the ship struck a reef, believed to be one of the Swain Group. All aboard were able to take to the brig's only two boats—a long-boat which held eleven people, and a pinnace with the remaining seven. The pinnace was delayed in making a getaway when it was found that the captain's nephew was missing. A search of the derelict revealed the boy on his knees in his cabin, praying.

The long-boat, whose occupants included the Frasers, proved to be unseaworthy, and continual bailing was necessary. Four days later Mrs Fraser (she was thirty-seven years old at the time) gave birth to a baby, which died shortly afterwards and was cast into the sea. Eventually the castaways in both boats landed on one of the Bunker Islands, and here the boatswain and six other seamen commandeered the pinnace and left for the mainland.

After taking a badly needed, but brief, rest and trying to do what little they could to make the leaking boat seaworthy, the eleven people decided to leave the security of their shelter to try also to reach the mainland, which Captain Fraser estimated was about fifty miles distant. For another two weeks they tossed hopelessly about in the patched-up long-boat, bailing endlessly and expecting any moment that the crazy craft would founder. They came ashore at Great Sandy Island, later to be renamed Fraser Island.

As to the seven men in the pinnace: they had landed on the mainland near Wilde Bay, and here were made prisoners of a tribe of natives who, after stripping them of their clothes and paltry possessions, made them work for them cutting wood and doing various odd jobs. Two of the captives, a British sailor and an American negro, made their escape one night and set off to walk to the Moreton Bay penal settlement. In this they were successful, and when they eventually reached their destination they told Lieutenant Otter, an officer of the detachment stationed at the settlement, their story.

Meanwhile the Fraser party had also attempted to walk to Moreton Bay, believing they were on the mainland. They, too, were captured by natives and were subjected to inhuman treatment, torture and in some cases death. Mrs Fraser saw her husband speared to death because, through illness, he was unable to work. She witnessed, too, the chief officer of the *Stirling Castle* being roasted alive over a slow fire.

Mrs Fraser's own treatment at the hands of her captors was no less fearful than that of the men. Some of her sufferings may be understood when reading Lieutenant Otter's report, after a rescue of the survivors had been effected. 'The woman,' he wrote, 'was a skeleton; the skin literally hung to her bones. Her legs were a mass of sores where the savages had tortured her with firebrands.... When we met her she had been for two days without food and had subsisted the most part of the time on a kind of fern root found in swamps. Now and then she would get the tail or fin of a fish when the savages had a superabundance, and then she was obliged to earn it by dragging heavy logs of wood and fetching water. She was not allowed in their shelters, but, naked as she was, she was obliged to lie out the whole night, even in the heaviest rains. This is but a slight sketch of what she went through. When we had got about halfway to our boats we were obliged to carry her. We did not arrive until next morning when she begged for hot water, as she was anxious to restore her face and person to a natural colour. The natives had rubbed her body every day with charcoal to darken her skin.'

When Lieutenant Otter organised the search party, on hearing the story of the captive castaways, a convict named John Graham offered his services and was accepted. Graham was an Irishman who had been transported to Botany Bay for seven years in 1824 for stealing 6 pounds of hemp. Later he was transferred to Moreton Bay, and while there took to the bush. In his wanderings he stumbled into an Aboriginal camp; he was treated kindly and lived with the tribe for nearly six years. Tiring of being so long absent from white company he decided to give himself up, and so he returned to the penal settlement. It was because of Graham's bushmanship and knowledge of the natives and their language that Lieutenant Otter decided to accept his services.

The rescue party eventually reached the white prisoners and Graham little difficulty in bringing in the men survivors— the second mate, John Baxter, and two ship's boys, Robert Carey and Robert Hanham. Mrs Fraser's rescue entailed much danger as the natives seemed determined to keep her. Lieutenant Otter said in his report: Graham shunned neither danger nor fatigue, and on the last occasion he was exposed to very imminent risk by venturing into a large camp where Mrs Fraser was detained.' The natives looked upon the white woman as a curiosity, hence their reason for wanting to keep her.

Afterwards, the commandant of the Moreton Bay penal settlement, Captain Foster Fyans, wrote: 'To Graham alone are we indebted for the recovery of Mrs Fraser.' Fyans sent Graham to Sydney where he was given a ticket-of-leave and £10 with which to start life afresh. There was a happy sequel to Mrs Fraser's great sorrows. She subsequently married Captain Greene, the commander of the vessel in which she sailed back to Britain from Sydney.

THE WRECK

> 'Turn out, boys'—'What's up with our super, tonight?
> The man's mad—two hours to daybreak I'd swear—
> Stark mad, why there isn't glimmer of light.'
> 'Take Bolingbroke, Alec, give Jack the young mare;
> Look sharp. A large vessel lies jamm'd on the reef,
> And many on board still, and some washed on shore.
> Ride straight with the news—they may send some relief
> From the township; and we can do little more.'

Adam Lindsay Gordon's poem 'The Wreck' is based upon a tragic sea disaster: the wreck of *Admella* near Cape Northumberland, South Australia. The *Admella* was a steamship of 360 tons built expressly for the Australian intercolonial trade. When she met her doom on the night of 9th August 1859, she had 113 people aboard; also 7 racehorses and a general cargo. Women and children were included in the passenger list.

Gordon's poem tells of the wild ride before dawn of station hands bearing news of the disaster to the Mount Gambier telegraph station. A telegram containing the tragic tidings was immediately dispatched to Melbourne, reading as follows:

Mount Gambier, Monday, 3.30 p.m.
I have just received intelligence from the head-keeper of the light-house at Cape Northumberland of the total wreck of the Admella steamer at, or near, the site of the wreck of the Nene Valley. Two of the crew (it is feared the only survivors) came to the lighthouse at 7 a.m. today. She went ashore at 5 a.m. on Saturday, and when they left a number of souls, including the Captain, were clinging to the wreck.

E. H. DERRINGTON,
Station Master.

Soon afterwards Melbourne received another telegram from Mount Gambier:

Mount Gambier. August 9.
A special message from Cape Northumberland brings further particulars. The Admella (says one of the two survivors) when she struck

156

was off her course, having been put before the wind while one of the racehorses on board was shifted, and having been again put on her course without allowance being made for leeway.

The weather was foggy at the time. The boats were washed adrift, and the quarter boat was lost through the carelessness of a passenger. It was last seen drifting out to sea, with a man astride the keel. If these boats could have been kept, there is every probability all hands would have been saved.

The ship broke into three pieces, and ropes were used to get people from one part to another. The second mate attempted to reach the shore by means of a lifebuoy, but was drowned in the surf.

The two survivors reached shore by means of a little raft they constructed out of a boom, and they were offered £500 by one of the passengers if they would carry him with them.

The scene was heart-rending; bodies floating round the wreck, passengers clinging to the hull and frantically offering money, jewels, everything they possessed to be carried safely ashore.

The Corio left Adelaide last night with the Government lifeboat.

E. H. DERRINGTON
Station Master.

The following day Sydney and Melbourne received telegrams from Adelaide as follows:

Adelaide, Tuesday.
Business is entirely suspended, all classes being engrossed by the wreck of the Admella. The portico of the Exchange was crowded all day with friends of the passengers, and great anxiety was shown to get the latest news by telegraph. The Corio was despatched to Cape Northumberland last night to render assistance if possible.

Both Houses of Parliament adjourned today, two sons of the President of the Council being among the passengers of the Admella.

From an Adelaide newspaper we learn of the attempts to rescue survivors of the wreck by the captain of the *Corio*.

'As early as possible after the receipt of the news on Monday, the Corio was fitted out in a hurried manner for the trip. On Wednesday she reached Cape Northumberland lighthouse, where a signal was made informing them the wreck was to windward; consequently, from not having received authentic information of its position, she had passed the wreck. It was not until 4.30 p.m. that she returned to the scene of the catastrophe.

'On reaching the reefs a heart-rending spectacle presented itself. A fresh breeze from the north-west whipped up a tremendous sea which was making a fair breach over the wreck, which consisted merely of the after-compartment from the taffrail to the break of the poop. This fragment was the only portion remaining of the ill-fated *Admella*, except some part of the boiler which at times was visible in the surf.

'The wreck had fallen over on the starboard side, and as the heavy rollers tumbled in they seemed with their foaming crests to threaten instant annihilation to the only hope on which depended the lives of so many human beings, who were seen moving about. Some climbed the mizen rigging and waved to us with half frantic energy. Although the sea that was running made it utterly impracticable to render the slightest assistance to them, yet we were able to proceed so near that the cries and shouts of the unfortunate people were distinctly heard.

'As night approached it was necessary to seek an offing, which was kept during a night of intense feeling preventing the idea of slumber from entering the minds of those on board the *Corio*. Next morning we steamed close to the reef, or within a furlong, and although the weather had somewhat moderated yet it was impossible to proceed to the rescue from seaward. Another obstacle presented itself in the evident unwillingness of the crew of the lifeboat to attempt the passage between the rocks. Lewis Thomas (coxswain) and Peter Smith, however, volunteered to make the attempt and the crew at once returned to their perilous duty and manned the boat.

'After two attempts she took the narrow passage stern foremost, and with a boiling sea around them proceeded through into comparatively smooth water between the reef and the sea beach surf. In this dangerous manoeuvre the boat was piloted by signals from the steamer, but after getting at the shore side of the reef no further progress was made. The crew was forced unwillingly to abandon the attempt, and beach the boat...'

In the meantime the *Lady Bird*, owned by the Henty Brothers of

Melbourne, had also arrived on the scene in an endeavour to bring rescue, but she, too, was helpless. Those people still clinging to the wreck were suffering bitterly from hunger, thirst, and exposure in the surging sea. After the third night none remained of the women and children on the fore part of the wreck. One by one they had become exhausted and dropped into the sea.

On 13th August, the seventh day of the wreck, a lifeboat managed to reach the survivors who now numbered nineteen. Only one woman was alive, a passenger named Miss Ledwith. Even so, their sufferings were not at an end; as they were being hauled through the surf by the aid of a line, the lifeboat capsized and one more life was lost.

In 1950, after I had recalled in an ABC radio programme the wreck of the *Admella*, I received a letter from a Mrs A. V. Gray, who was a daughter of the sole woman survivor. Mrs Gray was then in her late seventies. She said that her mother, who had died about thirty-three years previously in Ballarat at the age of seventy-seven, was just nineteen years old at the time of the tragedy. She was clad only in her night attire during the seven days' ordeal and, like the rest of the survivors, was without food or water. The only drink they had was when it rained and the men wrung the fresh water out of their shirts, which they had taken off to collect it.

THE CASTAWAYS

The South Pacific, vast ocean of mysteries, has produced a lengthy number of Crusoes. Many have been the misfortunes and trials of unfortunate castaways, one form of suffering being followed by another. The map of Oceania shows, far to the south and nearly two hundred miles from the southernmost point of New Zealand, the Auckland Islands. One of the group is a barren outpost of rock known as Disappointment Island. Fifteen men, survivors of a wrecked vessel who lived like Crusoes on its bare ground for nine bitter months, agreed that Disappointment Island was aptly named.

The sailing-vessel *Dundonald* was on her way from Australia to England when she crashed on the rocks of the island, in the early years of this century. The four-masted barque, loaded down with wheat, cleared Sydney Heads on 17th February 1907. It was during a violent storm which drove her off course that the vessel jammed into a great fissure in the cliffs. A gaunt needle of rock gashed a jagged hole in her bow, below the waterline, and held her fast.

As dawn broke, the handful of men clinging desperately to her yards found that the captain, his son, and ten others had been swept to death in the black nightmare of wind and rain. The ship was beginning to break up as the survivors carefully scrambled inch by inch along the jigger to the cliff-face and dragged themselves bruised and bleeding up to the cliff-top.

That day they held council and, after surveying the wreck of the *Dundonald*, the mate told them what he thought of their hopes of rescue.

'If she hadn't cracked up so quickly, we might have been able to rescue some stores. There isn't a hope, now—the deck is right under. The sails are the only things we've managed to salvage.'

'Whereabouts do you reckon we are, chief?' asked a sailor.

'Well, as you know, the gale over the last few days drove us right off our course. The atmospheric storms played merry hell with the compass. We were steering by dead reckoning alone there was no sun to take a bearing.

'I told the skipper that I was pretty worried that we might hit the Auckland Islands, and I pointed to them on the chart. The skipper said he thought we were at least forty miles to the windward of the group. "I hope I'm right," he said, "we don't want to end up in that graveyard of ships."

'Well, boys, I reckon that that's just where we are. And from my memory of studying the chart I'd say that this rocky dump is that part of the group called Disappointment Island.' There was silence for a moment before the mate continued. 'The island is no more than about two miles long by one and a half miles wide.'

'Blimey,' commented a sailor, 'there's not much chance then of finding any tucker—only those stinking mollyhawks. We'll have to eat 'em raw. Not one of us has a box of matches to light a fire.'

'Oh, don't give up hope,' said the mate trying to be optimistic. 'First of all let's look around the island. That won't take long; there's not that much of it. But I know for a fact that some of these islands have food depots on them. So many ships have come to grief in these latitudes that stores of food and clothes have been left on some of the islands. We may have struck it lucky. Who knows?'

Hopes were dashed when the castaways found that the island was a barren desolation without any sign of a food depot. So it was that the fifteen men were obliged to live on the rank, raw flesh of the mollyhawks that nested on the island in thousands. There was one bright spot. A couple of weeks after the disaster a seaman found a soaked box half-full of matches. As misers watch their gold, they guarded that handful of matches as they slowly dried in the sun. Several fires were lit and kept burning throughout the long winter months. From now on the survivors were able to dine on cooked mollyhawks.

One of the men, the second mate, kept a diary, recording events and the way they managed to exist. This is what he wrote after they had been marooned for fifty-five days: 'You should see us killing the mollyhawks. We are generally covered in blood. Everyone cooks his own bird. Mostly it is burnt on the outside and raw inside. It is so unpleasant cooking in the rain and snow that I, for one, intend building a cookhouse. Our hair is long and tangled. Some of us have breeches made of the sailcloth we salvaged from the wreck.'

Sure enough, the second mate built his cookhouse. It was a kind of underground hut in the form of a trench with a roof of sticks covered with bushes and earth. One end of it made a snug shelter through the bitter winter nights, the other end being used as a cookhouse. Others of the castaways followed his example, and soon there were many underground huts.

However, cooking underground had its disadvantages, according to this entry in the second mate's diary a few days later.

'By the time you have cooked your bird you are as black as a negro. All of us now look like savages. We wash ourselves in a strange manner, using the skins of the mollyhawks for towels. For soap we rub our faces with the greasy part of the bird, and then wipe with the feather side. We call it a skin wash.

'Although the cookhouse idea was hardly a success, it led to the accidental discovery of a method to make the wretched food palatable.

Last night one of the men forgot that he'd left a bird in his smoky cookhouse. This morning he found that it was smoked brown like a well-cured ham. It tasted better than the vile flavour these birds have, so from now on we'll have smoked mollyhawks.'

It was at this stage that the birds left the island on their annual migration, and the fifteen Crusoes were faced with a serious food problem. They discussed the situation and the other matter that was ever in their thoughts, the chances of rescue.

'Fortunately, boys,' the mate advised them, 'we have a few dozen smoked birds on hand. We'll dole them out and in the meantime see if we can clout a seal or two. It won't be easy, seeing that they seldom come ashore here.'

'How come there's been no ships looking for us?' he was asked. 'We've been here for 136 days, and in all that time we've only sighted one white speck on the horizon.'

'You don't have to remind us of that, Johnny,' the mate answered ruefully. 'We must have burnt nearly every bit of scrub on the island in the bonfire to attract attention. Whoever named this bit of rock Disappointment sure named it right. Maybe ships have been sent out to make a search, but they've given up by now.

'Anyway, it's no use getting downhearted. We all know it's hell, but we may yet get out of it. Look, this is a crazy idea I have in mind,' he continued, 'but unless we take a crazy chance there may be no hope for us. The island that we can see dimly through the mist can't be more than seven miles away. I'm positive we'd find a food depot on one of these islands, and maybe this might be the one.'

'But there's no timber on this ruddy rock. We'd have to build a boat to get to it,' interrupted one of his listeners.

'Yes, only bits of sticks and twigs from the stunted bushes', agreed the mate. 'But I suggest we try and lace the stuff into some kind of a rough wicker-work basket. We could use it as a framework to put canvas underneath. It should make a sort of floating cockleshell that might take two or three of us over to the island.'

'Blimey,' exclaimed someone. 'I'd rather try and swim there! And don't forget there's no more sailcloth left. It's all been cut up for breeches and blankets.'

The mate was not to be discouraged. 'We'll just have to give up our pants and blankets. They'll all have to be unpicked and sewn together again. We've still got plenty of bone needles, haven't we?'

'Sewing is not the problem,' spoke up another. 'What about oars? You can't use bone needles for oars, nor can you make 'em out of bits of twigs.'

'You're not telling me anything that I haven't realised,' the mate answered. 'I know it sounds crazy, but all we can do about oars is to make some sort of paddles of forked sticks with canvas tied round the forks.'

And so the men collected sticks and twigs from the scrub and made a ramshackle framework. The pieces of sailcloth were sewn into a jagged oval sheet and then stretched tightly over the frame. Incidentally, this crazy cockleshell may be seen today in the Canterbury Museum, New Zealand, serving as a memorial to the courage and ingenuity of the wrecked survivors of the *Dundonald*.

Three men, one of whom was an Australian, volunteered to brave the intervening miles of windswept sea to the nearest island to seek food for the rest. The incredible craft bobbed dizzily at the whim of every wave, but after hours of paddling it reached the island. The trio had with them two precious matches, the last remaining two on Disappointment Island, and with one of these they lit a fire to let their comrades know they had landed safely.

The island was a large one, and for days they plodded over range after range of hills clouded in dense forest and shrouded in mist. Their food was running low, and now they were deeply depressed at the thought of the dangerous return trip to Disappointment Island with the disheartening news of finding no food depot.

Suddenly they stopped, unable to believe their eyes. Before them was a painted notice: TO THE DEPOT. 4 miles. An arrow pointed down the creek through the scrub. The rest of the story is told in the second mate's diary.

'As days passed without the return of the voyagers, the rest of us on Disappointment Island gave them up for dead. Judge our joy when one day we saw them approaching the island not in the crazy craft but the most wonderful thing of all, a splendid seaworthy boat. We rushed down to meet them as they landed with a supply of food, clothes, a gun and ammunition, all of which were with the boat they had found in the food depot.

'The island they had reached was the main one of the group called Auckland Islands. Soon we all crossed over to this main island in our fine boat and settled there. Our food famine was at an end because apart from that found in the depot there were wild cattle on the nearby islands, and we were assured of plenty of fresh meat. We knew, too, that eventually a ship was sure to make a call.'

The castaways were there for but a few weeks when the *Hinemoa* with a party of scientific explorers dropped anchor off the island. Going ashore, the scientists were astonished to see the shipwrecked men and their Robinson Crusoe community. 'The castaways' community looked just like an African village,' one of the scientists wrote. 'As to the incredible craft in which they made the first journey to the island, it was truly unbelievable. That it reached its destination was a miracle.'

THE *LY-EE MOON* DISASTER

A strange memento of the wreck of the *Ly-ee Moon* could be seen for many years in the lighthouse at Green Cape, on the south coast of New South Wales. When the *Ly-ee Moon* crashed on the rocks at the foot of this lighthouse and broke in two, eighty lives were lost, including seven women. Coffins for the victims were sent by boat from the township of Eden, but one too many was sent and this was kept in the lighthouse for years afterwards.

A remarkable feature about the wreck was the tolling of the ship's bell as the passengers and crew were drowning. When the vessel broke in halves, one half was partly caught on a ledge and rocked to and fro, causing the bell to toll.

All the victims are buried in a little cleared space just below the lighthouse, but no memorial is erected there. It was originally intended to plant English firs round the burial ground as a memorial. A boatman was engaged to take the young trees from the town of Eden, but he ran into very rough weather and was forced to take shelter on the shores of Wonboyn Lake.

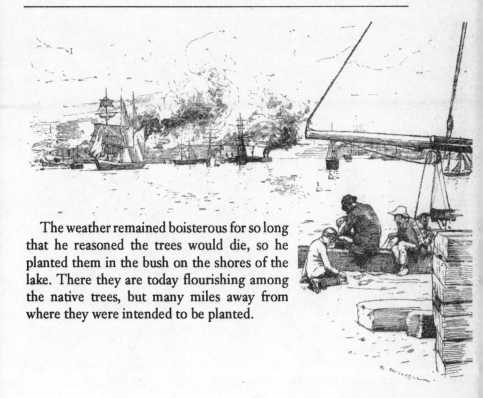

The weather remained boisterous for so long that he reasoned the trees would die, so he planted them in the bush on the shores of the lake. There they are today flourishing among the native trees, but many miles away from where they were intended to be planted.

ROGUES

The First Bushranger; Frank Gardiner's Last Exploit;
Prince of Pickpockets; The Convict Masquerader; King of the Cattle
Duffers; The Stolen Steamer; The Greatest Impostor in History;
Louis de Rougemont.

THE FIRST BUSHRANGER

The origin of the term 'bushranger' has been attributed to that pioneer of pioneers, Governor Phillip himself. Whether Phillip coined it or not, it is an apt description of Australia's earliest criminals. They were runaway convicts whose only shelter was in the bush and whose only resource was robbery. A man outside the law automatically became a

166

bushranger in the days when everything beyond the lines of the encampment on Sydney Cove was wild bush.

A memorial tablet in St James' Church, Sydney, is inscribed with a Latinised translation of the word bushranger. The memorial, which honours Dr Wardell—killed by bushrangers at Petersham, near Sydney, in 1834—states that he was killed by '*a latrone vagante*' (a wandering robber). With every man's hand raised against them, these escaped convicts were necessarily wanderers, and the only way they could live was by levying forcible contribution on isolated settlers.

The first bushranger of any note who made himself a nuisance to the small settlement on the shores of Sydney Cove was the big West Indian negro John Caesar, who had been transported to Botany Bay in the First Fleet under a sentence of seven years' penal servitude. His contemporaries usually referred to him as Julius Caesar; he took to the bush early in 1789. John Caesar's name is among a list of convicts published in Governor Phillips book *A Voyage to Botany Bay*, and from that same source we learn that he had been convicted at Maidstone, in Kent, and sentenced to seven years' transportation. There is no information as to the nature of his crime, but Captain David Collins, the Judge-Advocate, described him as 'black Caesar, a convict, and a savage of a darker hue'.

Soon after his arrival Caesar was sent to work in chains on Garden Island, where a few rough huts had been put up to accommodate a gang that was temporarily stationed there. None of the white prisoners were willing to share a hut with him and this affront, savouring of racial discrimination, seems to have given such mortal offence to the negro that he made up his mind to escape and become a freebooter, thus inaugurating the profession of bushranging as a peculiarly character-istic Australian one. When he cleared out, he took with him a musket, an iron pot, and a supply of rations—all very valuable commodities which would have been greatly missed from the limited resources of the settlement. He was not very long at large on this occasion, and when he was caught he was double-ironed and again relegated to Garden Island, where he had the reputation of being possessed of phenomenal bodily strength and of being a good worker. But it was not long before he once again made a break for liberty.

This time he secured a canoe and a good stock of provisions, and almost immediately began a series of robberies and depredations that kept the settlement in a state of constant excitement. He broke into the Commissariat Stores at Sydney, raided the vegetable garden at Garden Island, and robbed several settlers on the outskirts of the town. The first-named offence alone was sufficient to entitle him to 'a short shrift and a long rope' in the event of capture.

It seemed, however, that his misdeeds were taken for granted and no one made any effort to capture him, so the Governor was constrained to offer something that might move his subjects to an increase of energy in laying this slippery customer by the heels. A Government and General Order, of 29th January 1796, contains the following reference to our hero: 'The many robberies which have lately been committed render it necessary that some steps should be taken to put a stop to a practice so destructive of the happiness and comfort of the industrious. And as it is well known that a fellow known by the name of Black Caesar has absented himself some time past from his work, and has carried with him a musquet, notice is hereby given that whoever shall secure this man Black Caesar and bring him in with his arms shall receive as a reward five gallons of spirits.'

That the blood-money offered for the dark outlaw should have been rum was quite characteristic of those early days in New South Wales, and such an inducement could hardly have failed to be effective. It is not surprising to learn that Julius Caesar's career of brigandage was very speedily nipped in the bud.

It is probable that Caesar was blamed for many robberies that he did not commit. Every loss was set down as a score against him, and it is possible that many others made him the scapegoat for their own thieving. Collins says, 'Scarcely a morning arrived without a complaint being made to the magistrates of a loss of property supposed to have been occasioned by him. In fact, every theft that was committed was ascribed to him or some of the vagabonds who were in the woods, the number of whom at this time amounted to six or eight.'

The end of this early bushranger is recorded by Collins, writing in February 1796 thus: 'On the 15th a criminal court had met for the trial of two prisoners for a burglary, when information was received that

Black Caesar had that morning been shot by one Wimbow. This man and another, allured by the reward, had been for some days in quest of him. Finding his haunt, they concealed themselves all night at the edge of a bush, which they had perceived him enter in the dusk of the evening. In the morning he came out; when, looking round him and seeing his danger, he presented his musket; but before he could pull the trigger Wimbow fired and shot him, and he died in a few hours. Thus ended a man who certainly, during his life, could never have been estimated at more than one remove above the brute, and who had given more trouble than any other convict in the settlement.'

The Bengal rum had done its work.

Frank Gardiner's Last Exploit

Sunday, 15th June 1862, was a hot dusty day in the mid-west New South Wales township of Forbes. Preparations were under way for the departure of the Forbes gold escort for Sydney. Gold receiver James Parker handed the bags of gold to Inspector Charles Sanderson, who stacked them in a steel box and checked them.

'Twelve-ten, twelve-twenty, twelve-thirty. Total twelve-thirty, plus the Bank of New South Wales total of fourteen-eighty .... Naught, one, seven, two. That makes a grand total of 2,710 ounces. Correct! It's for my own peace of mind, Parker, that I like to recheck the gold and pack it myself. Then I don't mind accepting full responsibility for its departure from this end.'

A police sergeant from Sydney walked into the room. 'Good morning. Everything set for the road?'

'Yes, you can send your men in now,' said Sanderson. 'I hope you have a strong guard.'

'Oh, yes, I was told there'd be a hefty pile this trip.'

'Ten bags of gold plus £3,700 in notes. A tidy sum to tempt the hold-up boys. Your escort better keep their eyes skinned.'

'You can bet your life we'll watch every yard of the way. Not that I think there's much chance of us striking trouble. No sign of bush-rangers has been reported along the route.'

'You can't put much faith in reports. But good luck! I don't envy your trip in this wretched heat and dust.'

'The road couldn't be worse, pot-holes everywhere and the dust just about chokes you. Still, there's nothing we can do about the drought. I'll call the guard and we'll get cracking.

Oh, by the way,' added the sergeant, 'how is Sir Frederick Pottinger these days?'

'The chief is his usual pompous self.'

'How on earth a man so ill-fitted as Sir Frederick got the job of Chief of Police is beyond me.'

'Well, to the surprise of his friends and the amusement of his many critics he recently announced that he'd completed plans for the capture of Frank Gardiner!'

'What a joke!'

'As a matter of fact, a committee has been formed here in Forbes to give Sir Frederick a public dinner when the capture of Gardiner is effected. They've even sent to Sydney for a consignment of his favourite whisky for the celebration. It's expected any day now.'

The sergeant laughed uproariously. 'If Sir Frederick ever earns that grog, I'll eat my ruddy hat.'

The scene changes to the Eugowra Rocks area. About the same hour that the gold escort was leaving Forbes, teamster Michael O'Halloran was urging his bullocks along the dusty bush road. O'Halloran felt like a part of the road himself, covered as he was with red dust even in his mouth, eyes and nostrils. The leading bullocks had lurched too far on the offside toward the towering basalt rocks that gave the district its name, and he was trying to swing them back.

Suddenly a figure, garbed in a red shirt and wearing a dark cap pulled down on a charcoal-blackened face, stood in front of the teamster and pointed a rifle at him. 'Pull your bullocks across the road so that they block it!' came the command.

Michael O'Halloran looked defiantly at the man as he retorted, 'Go to blazes, ye black-faced divil!'

The man with the gun shook it menacingly. 'I said pull your bullocks across the road!'

'And I said, "Go to blazes!"' replied the teamster.

'Leave him to me,' interrupted another man who now appeared on

the scene. He was followed by five others, all of whom wore red shirts and had blackened faces like the man who had held up O'Halloran.

The one who had spoken last appeared to be the leader of the gang. 'Look, my Irish pal,' said he, 'we don't want to hurt you, or your team. All we want you to do is to pull them across the road, and leave them for an hour or two. You'll be well rewarded.'

'Seein' you're so persuasive, you and your black-faced minstrels, out of me way then, and I'll make me bullocks do what you bid!'

Whether, at this stage, the Irishman knew he was confronting Frank Gardiner and his gang, one can only surmise. As he backed up the animals with much shouting and chain-rattling, one of the bush-rangers exclaimed, 'Look what he's hauling. Rare Old Scotch. Open 'em up, boys! Are we in luck!'

Gardiner stood up. 'Easy on it, fellers. Steady now! No more than a good nip all round. When we're through, you can do what you like. But until the job's done, lay off it!' He turned to the Irishman. 'What about a swig for you, teamster?'

''Tis very generous you are, to be sure, with other people's property! I'll have ye know that the grog is a special consignment to honour the gentleman who'll soon be on your tails!'

'What do you mean, man? Pottinger?'

'The very same puffed-up bit of importance—Sir Frederick himself! And from what I hear, Frank Gardiner, he has you all tied up and bagged!' answered the teamster, looking the bushranger straight in the eye.

'So you know me.'

'Indade, I don't know ye, and I don't want to know ye! But, bedad, I know who ye are!'

Gardiner laughed. 'For all your cheek, Paddy, I don't think you'd turn informer—'

'Look, the signal! They've sighted the coach!' one of the gang called out.

Instantly Gardiner was on his feet. 'Behind the rocks, boys! Re-member again my orders: when you fire, don't aim to kill! You stay put, teamster. If you make an attempt to warn the coach, by thunder, I'll fill you with lead!'

It was just four o'clock in the afternoon, and the escort nearing Eugowra Rocks remarked that they were making pretty good time, considering the wretched state of the roads. They noticed the bullocky and team half-way across the track and thought he must have struck a bit of bother. As they neared him, they were obliged to slow down almost to a stop. A voice yelled 'Fire!' followed by a volley of shots.

Whinnying with fear, the coach horses reared and plunged in panic, while the driver with a bullet hole in his leg lost control of them. They bolted, but before they had gone a few yards the coach had overturned. The result was chaotic. The escort blazed away at the unseen outlaws who had the advantage of their concealment in the rocks. Seeing that resistance was useless, the escort threw down their guns when ordered. They looked incredulous when no less than fifteen members of Gardiner's gang descended from the Eugowra Rocks and proceeded to release the coach horses from the overturned vehicle, preparatory to removing the gold-boxes and coin.

They drank to their success, not forgetting to offer drinks to their captives before riding off. As they rode away, they warned the escort to make no attempt to follow them, otherwise they would be given more than a scare. It was a crestfallen group they addressed before taking to the scrub, yelling merrily.

The outlaws had cause to be jubilant, for their haul had been a valuable one. Advice of it transmitted to Gardiner, days previously by some of his many friends had been, as usual, most reliable. Among the motley population of Forbes, which in six months had grown from a grazing area to a mining town of twenty thousand, there were numerous folk who hated the police and passed on information of value to the bushrangers.

News of the hold-up stirred all Australia. The Premier of New South Wales announced in the Legislative Assembly that the Government was offering £1,000 for the apprehension of the bushrangers. He added that the Sydney trading banks had been asked to contribute pound for pound with the Government to make the reward much more attractive, but the banks had declined. Meanwhile the Police Chief, Sir Frederick Pottinger, was trying to justify his post by scouring the countryside with parties of police and black trackers. His efforts were not altogether futile for, although the gang had disbanded, five suspects were caught with some of the stolen money.

The trial of the five men was held in February 1863 at the Central Criminal Court. One of them, James Charters, aged twenty-four, arrested on suspicion, told this story in the course of his evidence:

'I was on my way to my sister's home near Forbes when I met Frank Gardiner and five other men. I knew Gardiner; I'd seen him several times before. He told me he was looking for help and asked me to join his camp. When I refused, he threatened me with a gun. I won't say he pointed the gun at me, but his hand went toward it. Well, I went off with the party.'

'Were these four other accused in the party?' the prosecutor asked.

'Three of them, sir,' replied Charters. 'Fordyce, Bow, and Manns. But not John Maguire. I never saw him at any time with the gang.'

'Proceed.'

'Well, we rode three days through the bush, never touching a road nor a town. When we wanted supplies, Gardiner would send a man into the nearest town.'

'Weren't you informed about these movements?' asked the prosecutor. 'Surely strict secrecy wasn't observed as to why you were kept with the gang?'

'I often wondered what it was all about, but every time I approached Gardiner he'd answer, "Wait and see." I felt something pretty bad would happen, but I swear I had no idea of the gang's intentions until we reached Eugowra Rocks.

'Before we arrived there Gardiner told us to take off our coats and put on red shirts, which I'd seen one of the men bring from a town the day before. Then we put on caps and blackened our faces with charcoal. We were then about half a mile from Eugowra Rocks. I didn't go any farther. I was told to mind some extra horses that the gang might need.

'About an hour later I heard shots from the direction of the Rocks, and soon after the gang came galloping up and we rode off to their hideout. The next day a lot of money was handed out, and they decided to split up.'

The jury said they did not need to hear any more. Fordyce, Bow, and

Manns were sentenced to death and hanged. Maguire was acquitted as was also Charters.

The gang's notorious leader and his close companions escaped the police search. Two years later Gardiner was discovered near Rockhampton living under his proper name of Christie. When arrested, he was the owner of a hotel and store. Brought back to Sydney to stand trial, Chief justice Stephens, apparently influenced by public sympathy, sentenced him to thirty-two years' hard labour.

The 'King of the Bushrangers' proved a model prisoner and was released after serving only ten years, on condition that he left the country. He ended his days in San Francisco, the only bushranger buried outside Australia.

In his memoirs of the Sydney of more than a century ago, the late Captain Charles wrote: 'I remember when I first came out seeing two boys shooting marbles in Argyle Street. One was a pleasant, fair-headed boy; the other a bright, round-headed youngster. I accidentally kicked one of the marbles, and recollect putting my hand on the fair boy's head and saying I was sorry. He looked up and smiled, and said it was all right. That same boy grew up to be the notorious bushranger, Frank Gardiner. The other lad became none other than the distinguished statesman and barrister, William Bede Dalley.'

By a strange fate, or the eternal fitness of things, Dalley defended Gardiner at his trial.

Prince of Pickpockets

Handsome George Barrington, one of the most dashing young blades of eighteenth-century London, was for more than fifteen years the most notorious thief in Great Britain. At Parramatta, New South Wales, lie the mortal remains of this prince of pickpockets, but neither his real name nor the place or date of his birth is definitely known. It is fairly certain that he was born near Dublin about 1755, reputedly the offspring of a certain Captain Barrington and a Mrs Waldron. After attending the blue-coat school in Dublin, he was apprenticed to an apothecary in that city. Always a likeable rascal, he attracted the attention of a clergyman of the Church of Ireland, Dr Westropp, who sent him at his own expense to a select grammar school with the intention of finishing his education at Trinity College.

Some months after his enrolment Barrington had a fight with a much bigger boy; and when he found his opponent getting the best of it he pulled out a penknife and stabbed him in the chest. When the schoolmaster flogged him, Barrington stole his watch together with twelve guineas and cleared out. Then about sixteen years of age, he joined a theatrical company—a travelling troupe—in which his small acting roles were to prove of considerable value when he turned his talents to professional pickpocketing.

Establishing himself in the most fashionable area of London, the young Barrington dressed elegantly and with his impeccable manners moved in the right circles, charming society leaders with his company. For years no one dreamt that Barrington, who was believed to be of noble lineage, was earning his income as a pickpocket. Drury Lane and other theatres were his favourite haunts, but he was always present as a member of the aristocratic audience.

It was a gala performance at Covent Garden that first unmasked the gentleman pickpocket. Most of fashionable London were present, including the visiting Russian Count Gregory Orloff and, of course, dear Mr Barrington. While conversing with the wealthy visitor he neatly extracted the count's diamond studded snuff-box. Although Barrington used his practised skill, Orloff detected the sleight-of-hand movement and shouted for help. Amid the consternation Barrington managed to slip the snuff-box back into Orloff's pocket; nevertheless he was charged and arrested. At his trial Orloff declined to appear and Barrington was acquitted, asserting that the whole incident had been an unhappy mistake.

Although it caused a certain amount of gossip, Barrington was accepted back in the ranks of high society and three months later, like every other man of quality and fashion in London, received a gold-crested invitation to the King's levee at St James's Palace. There, while in conversation with the Earl of Mexborough, Barrington ingeniously cut away his Order of the Garter with its nineteen large diamonds. The Earl did not discover his loss until he returned home, and there was no proof at the time of the thief's identity.

It was a woman who sent Barrington to his first prison. He had been

seen stealing her purse at a Drury Lane performance, and the lady had no pocket where he could slip it back when she accused him of the theft. When he was sentenced to three years in the hulks on the Thames, the *London Chronicle* sympathetically commented: 'He is the genteelest thief ever remembered at the Old Bailey. It is a great pity that he should be condemned to so vulgar an employment as heaving ballast.'

George Barrington did not have to descend to vulgar employment. His glib tongue and courtly manners enabled him to be relieved of heavy work on the hulks, and he was released after serving only one year's imprisonment. However, his fingers must have lost some of their dexterity during his detention, because he was arrested shortly afterwards with a stolen watch in his hat. This time he was sentenced to five years' imprisonment, but the magistrates were so moved by the rogue's eloquence, together with the excellent report of his behaviour while on the hulks, that he was released on condition that he stayed out of England.

Returning to his native land, the elegant Barrington practised his pickpocket profession among the Irish gentry for some time before moving to Scotland, but he found the pickings from the Celts less remunerative than those to which he was accustomed. Defying his banishment order, he made his way back to England where at the Chester fair he gathered loot to the value of £600. In 1790 he was caught stealing a gentleman's valuable gold watch, and he realised that he would need all the powers of his acting and eloquence to sway the judges this time.

'If I am acquitted,' he hopefully addressed the Bench, 'I will retire to some distant land where my name and misfortunes will be alike unknown. Harmless manners shall shield me from the reputation of guilt. Prejudice will not be able to misrepresent. I feel a cheerful hope, even at this awful moment, that the rest of my life will be conducted as to make me as much an object of esteemed applause as I am now the unhappy object of censure and suspicion.'

The judges were in full agreement with his suggestion that he would be better off in a distant country, and there was none more distant than Botany Bay. Nevertheless, if Barrington did not anticipate such far-off banishment, he was sentenced to only seven years' transportation, despite what Baron Eyre, the judge before whom he had appeared previously, said: 'This ought to have been a capital indictment, and it ought to have reached your life; and public justice very much calls for such a sacrifice. I cannot entertain the least hope that you will reform.'

Barrington was transported on the *Active*, which arrived at Sydney Cove on 26th September 1791. Apparently on the principle that it is wise to set a thief to catch a thief, Governor Phillip appointed him as a watchman at Parramatta. Within months he was promoted to the post of principal of the nightwatch and given a conditional pardon together with a land grant of thirty acres. A year before his term of exile was served, Governor Hunter, the new administrator, gave him an absolute pardon and made him chief constable of Parramatta. With this new appointment he received a good salary plus a further land grant of a hundred acres. Governor Hunter described him as 'one of the most zealous on public duty and one of the most exemplary in private life as any within the colony.'

In many works published since the early nineteenth century referring to Australian drama, George Barrington has been named as either the author or narrator (or both) of the famous prologue to the convict players' presentation of *The Revenge* in Sydney in 1796. There can be few Australians unfamiliar with its opening lines:

> *From distant climes o'er widespread seas we come,*
> *Though not with much eclat or beat of drum,*
> *True patriots all; for, be it understood,*
> *We left our country for our country's good;*
> *No private views disgrac'd our generous zeal,*
> *What urg'd our travels was our country's weal;*
> *And none will doubt but that our emigration*
> *Has prov'd most useful to the British nation.*

Barrington was not the author of the celebrated prologue, nor did he ever claim authorship. It was an adaptation of one of the *Original Poems* by Henry Carter of Leicester. Moreover, there is no real evidence that Barrington was the narrator of the lines when the convict players made their début.

A whole series of books were printed in London, purporting to describe Barrington's voyage to New South Wales, the history of the colony, and his own life there. Most, if not all, are simple forgeries; Barrington himself is reliably reputed to have disclaimed authorship. However, all these things, together with the remembrance of the light sentences imposed by his judges and the indulgences granted him by colonial governors, indicate that George Barrington was a man of remarkable personality and no small influence. Nor can there be any doubt that his reformation was genuine.

THE CONVICT MASQUERADER

One morning in the year 1833 Attorney David Chambers, an obscure Sydney lawyer, was seated in a shabby little office in Pitt Street which he shared with another lawyer. After reading a letter he had just received, he could not contain his joy.

'Charles, this is a stroke of luck! A letter signed by Henry, Viscount Lascelles. He wants me to prepare a power of attorney for a friend in England to receive £130,000 from his father, the Earl of Harewood. What a commission! To say nothing of the prestige it will bring me.'

His colleague congratulated him, and asked, 'Have you had any contact with Lord Lascelles?'

'No,' answered Chambers, 'I've never met his Lordship. Someone must have recommended my services to him, but I'm at a loss to know who might be that person. All that I know about Lord Lascelles is what I've been reading about him in the *Gazette* and the *Monitor*.'

'Yes, both newspapers vie with each other in reporting his social doings. His arrival has caused quite a stir in the colony. I believe he's an eligible bachelor. Certainly he's being entertained handsomely. I must confess, though,' added the lawyer thoughtfully, 'that his visit to the colony seems rather vague. He's accompanied by an Irish valet, but you wouldn't think he'd come to this outlandish part of the world on a pleasure trip.'

Attorney David Chambers agreed, but then he recalled seeing a paragraph in the *Gazette* stating that Governor Bourke had granted the distinguished visitor facilities to visit the penal settlements in New South Wales and Van Dieman's Land. 'Perhaps,' said Chambers, 'he is on an unofficial visit to make a report to the British Government on the convict system. Anyway, I should shortly know all about his affairs.'

The happy attorney was soon attending to his Lordship's wishes and duly drew up the legal papers. A few months later he received a shock when he opened a letter of reply from the London solicitors to whom he had addressed Lord Lascelles' documents. The London legal firm said that there was a grave mistake in the matter. They enclosed a brief letter from the Earl of Harewood in which he said, 'I am the only Lord Henry Lascelles. My eldest son and heir, Viscount Edward, is at present in Munich.'

The attorney was bewildered. Then he remembered that he possessed a copy of *Burke's Peerage*. Quickly he rummaged for the volume and, finding it hastily, turned up the long entry devoted to the Lascelles family. All the particulars were clearly given, but there was no mention of the younger so-called Henry Lascelles. With a groan the attorney grabbed his hat and made straight to the place where Lascelles was staying. It was a heavy hearted attorney who returned to his office and told the sad story to his legal friend.

'When I produced the London letter and the volume of *Burke's Peerage*, he wasn't perturbed in the slightest. He just dismissed it all with a smile, and said that there was some mistake and he would write immediately to his father and have the matter straightened out. To tell you the truth, he acted in such a convincing manner that I came away more or less believing that it was all a genuine error. But on my way here I met the court bailiff and he tipped me that a warrant is being issued for the swindler's arrest. He's being indicted as John Dow, alias Luttrell, charged with forging a promissory note.'

When the rogue calling himself Lord Lascelles was brought to trial, sensational evidence came to light. The prosecution called a number of convicts who had travelled to Van Diemen's Land with the prisoner nine years earlier in a convict ship when he was known as Dow. Among the many people who gave evidence as to how the ex-convict had duped them was Francis Prendergass of Windsor.

'The impostor came to my farm,' said Prendergass, 'and told me he was looking for a bit of good horseflesh for riding. I sold him three

181

horses, a saddle and a bridle for £50. He gave me a promissory note, a worthless bit of paper, in exchange. He called himself a lord, and I thought by the swag of gold he was wearing across his waistcoat that everything was all right.'

Continuing his evidence, Prendergass said, 'He and that other villain he called his Irish servant stayed at my farm for fifteen days. They ate my turkeys, fowls and ducks; and they wouldn't sit with me and my family at the same table. Oh, dear no, we weren't good enough for his Lordship and his manservant. The two of them sat at the dining-table in state, using my best linen and silver. And drinking my brandy, too!'

An excited stir was apparent in the Court when the impostor entered the box to defend himself. With the air of an aggrieved, but dignified member of the aristocracy, he 'explained' his predicament.

'I refuse to answer to the name of Dow or any other such alias. My name is Lascelles—Henry, Viscount Lascelles. I was sent to these colonies unknown to my father, the Earl of Harewood. I arrived in Van Diemen's Land as a convict in a strange land, destitute and penniless. My crime was simply a small gambling debt which I was unable to settle. Rather than have any stain on my illustrious family name, I called myself Dow. It was under this name that I was charged in London and transported as a convict.

'Having served my sentence in Van Diemen's Land, I reverted to my rightful name and title. After my conviction I wrote to my father imploring his forgiveness, but he did not reply. This is all a horrible tragic mistake.'

The Court, however, thought it was horrible, outright villainy. Judge Barton, before passing sentence, castigated the rogue in no uncertain terms and expressed his sympathy with the noble British family whose honour the masquerader had endeavoured to traduce. The whole colony, especially the social ladies smarting under the way they had been so thoroughly duped, were in full accord with the sentence—imprisonment for life.

KING OF THE CATTLE DUFFERS
Corella cattle station in the Northern Territory was once owned by

Harry Bedford, the King of the Cattle Duffers. At the age of sixty he was drowned in attempting to swim the flooded Corella Creek. That was thirty-one years after his incredible duffing deed, and twenty years after it had been immortalised by Rolf Boldrewood in the character of Starlight in his classic *Robbery Under Arms*.

The world's champion cattle-stealer, who 'lifted' 1,000 head of cattle at one go, was born in the Hawkesbury River district of New South Wales in 1842. He developed into a massively built youth, 6 feet 3 inches tall and proportioned like Hercules. As he grew older, his big physique was matched by his big ideas. He was a bushman born and bred, a superb horseman, and always on his wanderings he kept his eye open for the big opportunity.

Migrating from the Hawkesbury, Bedford travelled north to Queensland, working mainly as a stockman and drover. At the age of twenty-eight he was employed as a teamster driving drays from Tamba to Bowen Downs station, one of the largest cattle stations in Australia. One day he was talking to a couple of fellow teamsters, airing his opinion about station owners and the wealth they amassed. Warming up to his subject, he said they just sat back and watched their herds of cattle grow bigger and their bank-rolls get fatter. But did they ever do a day's work themselves? Of course not! They left it to the mugs their employees.

His listeners agreed and complained about their 'long hours and lousy wages'. One of the teamsters, talking about Morehead and Young, the owners of Bowen Downs station, reckoned they were just bloated capitalists and that they had so many cattle they wouldn't even know if they were 1,000 short on a muster.

'Of course they wouldn't!' agreed Redford. 'There must be over 60,000 here at Bowen Downs.' He paused before making the startling suggestion, 'Blimey, boys, why not help ourselves to a thousand.'

'You mean pinch a thousand head of cattle?' asked one of the incredulous teamsters.

'I do,' answered Redford unhesitatingly' 'The money we get selling them to be equally divided among us.'

Up spoke another. 'Bedford, you're crazy! You're forgetting the little matter of branding. All of the Bowen Downs cattle are branded.

Only a fool would try to sell duffed cattle with that brand anywhere in Queensland. Why, the brand is well known even in New South Wales.'

Bedford grinned broadly. 'Quite so,' he explained. 'But we'll take 'em farther afield! We'll drove 'em overland to South Australia, where the brand isn't known!'

There was a stunned silence before his listeners started on him hot and strong. South Australia was 1,000 miles away! Such an impossible droving feat had never been done before! There were no stations in between all the way, and nobody lived in those parts except wild natives! Why, they'd have to cross the country that stopped Burke and Wills, and *they* had a properly equipped expedition!

Harry Redford waited patiently until their outbursts had finished and then blithely replied. 'I know all that. We'd have to take our chance of finding feed and water all the way. But,' he continued with enthusiasm, 'it's a sporting chance! If we get the mob through to South Australia, we'll all be rich men.' He could see he was holding their interest as he told them, 'I've spent my life in the bush and, if you come with me, I reckon I could make it. We could travel down the Thompson River to the Barcoo, then down Cooper's Creek to the border. Of course we'd have to get the mob well away before mustering time. Now this is what I plan to do. We'd first...'

The other teamsters, won over by Redford's glib tongue and secure in the knowledge of his undoubted bushmanship, agreed to take part in the audacious project. No suspicion was aroused by the movement of the Tamba teamsters on Bowen Downs. There was nothing unusual if they were seen camped with their drays alongside a waterhole. If they were noticed riding about the property at times, they could be looking perhaps for some of their own strayed working bullocks. And so the cattle duffers casually collected small lots of beasts and moved them to an isolated gully with plenty of feed and water.

Then began the amazing transcontinental droving drama with a mob of 1,000 cattle on the move across grim, unknown country. It was not long before they were beyond the limits of pastoral occupation. Two hundred miles south of their starting-point they reached the Barcoo River, and here they rested for a brief respite. Ahead lay the uninhabited, terrible country where the explorers Burke and Wills perished. Undeterred by thoughts of that tragedy which had occurred only ten years previously, the duffers kept their mob moving.

In the normal dry season this territory would have been quite impassable for such a big mob of cattle, but luck was on the side of the reckless rogues, and water and herbage were obtainable. Five months after the incredible trek had begun they came in sight of Blanchewater station, near Lake Callabonna, in South Australia. Bedford had succeeded.

The world's number one cattle duffer blandly introduced himself to the station manager as Mr Collins, droving a mob belonging to himself and his brother overland to the Port Augusta saleyards. The manager told him that he could scarcely believe his eyes when he first saw the cloud of dust on the horizon. Then he was positive it was a mirage of a big mob of cattle coming from the direction of that no-man's land.

Mr Collins admitted that he did feel a little proud of being the first man to drove cattle across that territory.

185

'Oh, you're too modest!' exclaimed the manager. 'A thousand miles! Why, it was a remarkable achievement to cross that god forsaken country without any mob. But with 1,000 head of cattle it was a miracle!'

Anxious to get to business, Bedford remarked, 'Anyway, the cattle are none the worse for it. You can see they're in splendid condition.'

'Yes,' agreed the manager, 'I've been admiring them. The good season we've been having around these parts must have extended into the desert country. Your Queensland cattle seem superior to our South Australian stock. You should get a good price for them when you get down to the saleyards.'

Bedford was not boasting when he said, 'There isn't better stock in all Queensland. Then he assumed a confidential manner when he added, 'To be truthful, though, the boys and myself are tired of travelling. It's still a few hundred miles to the Port Augusta saleyards, and I'm anxious to return to my property. It's too much for my brother to manage on his own. You see, I've already been away for five months. If I get any reasonable offer for the cattle, I won't wait for the Port Augusta sales.'

The bait was swallowed. 'As a matter of fact, Mr Collins,' said the station manager, 'I'm very interested in your cattle. Maybe we can do business right now. Would you be satisfied with £5 a head? You probably would not do much better than that at the saleyards.'

Mr Collins agreed, and the deal was sealed with a draft made out in his favour for £5,000 on the Bank of Adelaide. The duffers lost no time in making for Adelaide where they cashed the draft and divided it equally among the three of them.

Back in far-off Queensland the stockmen on Bowen Downs station had begun the annual mustering. It took two months to complete the big job of counting the cattle. Bill Butler, the overseer, lost his temper when he looked at the figures. He reckoned the men had been careless in the counting; who was to blame for the mistake he didn't know, but it all had to be done again. There was no mistake, as the checking proved. A thousand head of cattle were missing!

Looking for clues, the station blackboys tracked their way to the hidden stockyards in the Thompson River gully. From there they traced the tracks for miles down river and out toward the never-never country. The police were notified, extensive inquiries made, and it was found that missing also were Harry Bedford and two other teamsters.

Eventually the South Australian police learnt that the manager of Blanchewater station had lately purchased 1,000 head of Queensland cattle from a Mr Harry Collins who was accompanied by two other drovers. Immediately, a warrant was issued for the arrest of Harry Bedford, alias Collins, and his two mates. The latter were never found. Bedford was traced to New South Wales, where he was arrested and charged in February 1871.

It took twelve months for the Crown to collect all the evidence against the ace of all cattle duffers, during which time he was held as a prisoner on remand. When the preparations for the trial were at last completed, the case came before Mr justice Blakeney at the town of Roma, Western Queensland. The body of the court was packed to capacity with bushmen who listened with rapt attention to the story of the world's greatest cattle-duffing exploit.

In the course of his summing-up His Honour said to the jury, 'Remember, this is a major crime for which the prisoner is being tried. Do not allow your admiration for a remarkable feat of bushmanship to outweigh a gross and flagrant breach of law and order. One thousand head of cattle were stolen and sold to Mr Mules of Blanchewater station for £5,000. Mr Mules has identified the prisoner as the man who sold him the cattle. The receipt for the bank draft has been identified with the writing of the accused. Gentlemen, the case against the prisoner is very, very plain.'

As His Honour expected, the jury spent little time in reaching their verdict. They announced it to the accompaniment of cheers and dapping—NOT GUILTY. Livid with rage, Judge Blakeney called for silence. With a supreme effort he stifled his intense anger and, turning to the members of the jury, he calmly but meaningly remarked, 'I thank God, gentlemen, that the verdict is yours—not mine!'

Judge Blakeney made a scathing report of the jurors to the Government and, as a result, a proclamation was issued by the Governor of Queensland declaring and ordering, 'The criminal jurisdiction possessed by the District Court at Roma shall be withdrawn therefrom for the term of two years.'

After his acquittal Redford left for North Australia, there to remain and prosper until his death.

The Stolen Steamer

On an October morning in 1880 a well-dressed and opulent looking gentleman was shown into the manager's office of one of the leading ship chandlers in Glasgow.

'Please be seated, sir,' said the manager. 'I see by your card, Mr Walker, that you are a broker.'

The visitor nodded. 'My business with you is this: I'm acting as broker for Mr Eric Smith, nephew of W. H. Smith who, as you may know, was until recent years First Lord of the Admiralty.' The name of that distinguished gentleman was not unknown to the manager.

'He's a very dear friend of mine,' continued the visitor. 'Unfortunately his health has not been the best lately, and he thinks a long sea voyage may do him good.'

'A sea trip often works wonders, Mr Walker.'

'As you say. Well, he's asked me to accompany him on a world tour. Acting on his instructions, I've chartered the steamer *Ferret* from the Highland Company.'

'*Chartered* the steamer?' The manager was incredulous.

'Oh, you must remember that my friend and client is a man of great wealth. He would not be happy travelling on a steamer with other passengers, so it's better for him to charter the vessel seeing that he's in the position to do so.

Mr Walker got down to business. 'Here are the ship's papers and documents from the owners, which you will see have been signed and sealed. Everything has been finalised. Would you please examine them?'

The manager could see at a glance that all the papers were in order. Moreover, his firm did much business with the Highland Company. He assured the visitor that he would be happy to outfit the *Ferret* with whatever was required.

'It's merely a matter of stores for the steamer that I'm concerned with at the moment. I should think we would need about £1,500 worth.'

'With pleasure, Mr Walker. Come with me to the chief stores clerk. There we can make out a list of your requirements.' He asked when the ship would be leaving.

'Not for four months. We don't want to rush things. But it's better to have all the preliminaries attended to and the stores taken aboard, and the accounts paid.' Then he added, 'As soon as you let me have your account, I'll draw up a cheque at the usual ninety days.'

During the next three months Walker and his friend Smith, who called himself the nephew of the former Lord of the Admiralty, stayed in Glasgow. There they were given lavish hospitality by merchants and business men.

Shortly before the ninety-day period of the bill of costs was due, the two gentlemen and the ship vanished. Nevertheless nothing was suspected until the firm of chandlers presented their bill for payment and was told it was dishonoured. Other business firms had been duped, and now these merchants met together to assess their total losses and lament over their misfortunes. The references produced by the two swindlers were found to be false; Smith, as he called himself, was no relation to the Lord of the Admiralty, and not one of the important people Walker so glibly called his friends had heard of him. But if the merchants' losses were big, the Highland Shipping Company had suffered much greater misfortune. They had been robbed of a steamer worth £100,000.

On the very morning that the great swindle was discovered, the police received a telegram from Cardiff saying that the *Ferret* had called there, filled her bunkers with coal and, after paying for it with worthless bills, sailed away. The *Ferret*'s owners could only console themselves with the thought that she would have to put into another seaport sooner or later, and that every port authority in the world would be on the lookout for the stolen steamer.

In the meantime the SS *Ferret* was on the high seas. Her commander, Captain Wright, was in league with the two swindlers but, apparently, the crew thought that everything was in shipshape order. At any rate they swore later that the first information they received regarding the mysterious voyage was soon after they left Cardiff.

According to the crew, Walker called them together in the messroom and told them a fantastic tale. He began by saying that not only would every man be paid double rates, as promised when they were signed on, but each would receive a handsome bonus at the end of the voyage. He explained that the vessel was on a government mission and that there were certain conditions that must he strictly observed. No one must go ashore at any port of call, whatever the circumstances. 'We are on a government mission and pledged to secrecy,' he told the crew. 'At the moment I'm unable to divulge our destination. Suffice to say that Mr Smith, who is travelling incognito, is one of America's most important diplomats.'

Walker explained that Mr Smith, because of political intrigue, was being sought by foreign spies. The British Government had arranged to spirit him away on the *Ferret*, and it was the solemn duty of everyone aboard the vessel to help confuse and confound the enemy spies in every possible manner. Alas, he added, despite all the planning and secrecy, the commander of the vessel had just received cable advice in code to the effect that foreign agents had been warned to watch out for the *Ferret* when it made port.

All was not lost, according to Walker; indeed the enemy would be tricked with a master stroke. A bogus shipwreck would be staged when the vessel entered Mediterranean waters. Firstly a fake SOS message would be sent, and then various articles and parts of the steamer were to be thrown overboard in the hope that they would be washed ashore.

Lifebuoys with the name *Ferret* would be included. 'Then we'll sneak into an out-of-the-way anchorage, repaint the ship, make some alterations to her appearance, and change her name. There'll be no worries after that.'

Walker looked at the astounded faces of the crew and he dismissed them. 'That's all for now, men. Remember to keep your mouths shut, and the USA Government will make it well worth your while.'

What was the motive of the swindlers? Simply this: they intended trading in stolen cargo and, in fact, contemplated piracy. Lloyds of London and the British Board of Trade had, of course, notified every shipping agent and every British Consul in overseas ports to watch closely for the stolen steamer. Naturally the swindlers had anticipated all this and arranged with an accomplice to inform them by cable of the latest developments. The cable messages were sent in code.

Their plans were so far successful. After the faked shipwreck and the changing of the ship's name they sailed to Cape Verde and bought goods with a bogus bill negotiable in London. Then to Santos where they made known that they were on their way to Marseilles and were willing to accept cargo. One firm loaded them with 4,000 bags of coffee worth £10 a bag. But the rogues sailed instead to Cape Town, where they sold the coffee cargo for the bargain price of £20,000.

One might well ask how all this was explained to the crew. It was not long before they realised they had been hoodwinked. Here is what a member of the crew had to say about the astonishing story in the course of evidence he gave at a later date:

'In the beginning we believed their tale about the ship being on a government mission and that they were acting on instructions from the secret service. They told us to change our names; also that Walker was to be called Wallace, Smith was to be known as Henderson, but Wright, the captain, would keep his own name.

'Soon we realised there was something fishy about it all. We demanded a showdown, but the three of them threatened and forced us into submission. They admitted they were swindlers and said that, if they were caught, they would swear we were willing accomplices.

'Before going to Australia we called at Gibraltar, Malta, Cape Verde, Santos, and Mauritius. The steamer was repainted and renamed many times, and was always disguised with various alterations made to the upper decks. The last renaming was at Mauritius. There the steamer was docked, cleaned and repainted, and the name altered to SS *India*.

'Whenever we anchored in port, none of us dared to go ashore. The captain stayed on the bridge and we always had steam up ready to slip out at a moment's notice. It was rumoured that when we got into Australian waters, plans had been made for turning the vessel into an armed privateer to attack ships carrying gold from the diggings.'

The incredible career of the steamer *Ferret* came to an end in Melbourne. Her capture was due to the vigilance of a keen-eyed customs officer who drew the attention to his chief of the vessel lying at anchor in Port Phillip.

'That steamer has been puzzling me,' he told him. 'She's always with steam up, ready to sail. Nobody has ever sighted any member of her crew ashore; nor has the captain been seen. It set me thinking. I got so curious that I searched our shipping records, but there was no mention of any steamer named *India* that looked anything like her. Then I had an idea. I looked up the descriptions of missing vessels. Hell's bells, guess what! She resembles the *Ferret!* The stolen steamer that was supposed to have been wrecked with all hands. Although a few bits of wreckage with the name *Ferret* were picked up, no bodies were found. It was all pretty suspicious. This may be her!'

The Melbourne Port authorities made plans and quietly raided the mystery vessel. The three swindlers, however, were not on board. A thorough search revealed how well all traces of the name *Ferret* had been removed; nevertheless a small sheet of paper with the original name printed on it was found inside a book. Also were found a printing-press, postage stamps of many countries, and incriminating messages in code sent and received by the stolen steamer. In any case the crew admitted everything.

Then began the hunt for the master thieves. Captain Wright was the first to be caught when he became involved in a drunken brawl in Melbourne. On his arrest his true identity was established. Soon afterwards Smith was caught, and eventually Walker was arrested at the Victorian town of Wodonga. All three were brought to trial and found guilty, but their sentences were astonishingly light considering their colossal frauds. Walker and Smith got seven years' hard labour and Captain Wright three years' hard labour.

THE GREATEST IMPOSTOR IN HISTORY

Not without justification was Arthur Orton described as 'the greatest impostor in history'. The twenty-four-stone butcher from Wagga Wagga was also termed 'a vast carcass lumbering the earth with lies'. His widow who lived until 1926, twenty-eight years after his death, always declared with an air of superiority that he was none of these things, but was undoubtedly the English baronet Sir Roger Tichborne. If anyone had the temerity to remind her that her husband, after he had been sentenced to fourteen years' imprisonment, had published a full confession of his guilt as an impostor, she would have none of it. Mrs Orton was determined to regard herself as the widow of a baronet.

The story begins when Sir Roger Tichborne, Bart, heir to the estates of a wealthy English family in Hampshire, was drowned when the ship *Bella* was wrecked near Rio de Janeiro in 1854. All those aboard the vessel lost their lives, and although Sir Roger's body was not found he was presumed dead. Although there is no possible doubt that the youthful baronet was drowned, his mother, the dowager Lady Tichborne, refused to believe it and repeatedly advertised for news of him in newspapers throughout the world. The eccentric Lady Tichborne was of French descent, 'a spoiled beauty, impulsive and self-willed, but essentially weak and visionary', and because of her character was the basic cause of all the disastrous trouble that was to come to the Tichborne family.

One of the advertisements Lady Tichborne inserted in a Sydney newspaper was seen by Arthur Orton at his butchery business in Wagga Wagga, where he was trading under the name of Thomas Castro. Orton was born in Wapping, London, in 1834 (five years after the birth of Sir Roger Tichborne), and at the age of fourteen went to sea on a ship bound for Chile. Disliking his experience, he deserted the vessel at Valparaiso and lived some time there before migrating to Australia.

At the time when Orton read the Missing Persons advertisement he was in financial difficulties and trying to stave off creditors. The corpulent rogue decided that, by posing as the missing Sir Roger, his monetary problems might be solved or at least kept in abeyance. At any rate he saw a solicitor and 'admitted' that he was the missing heir. There had always been an air of mystery about 'Thomas Castro' and, to be sure, he had told of living in South America, so when the news of the claimant spread around the district his creditors told him not to worry about his debts—they were willing to advance him as much credit as he needed.

At this stage Orton was merely counting on obtaining a few pounds from Lady Tichborne while his credentials were being investigated, and probably never thought that he would be accepted as Sir Roger. He could scarcely have hoped to dupe her ladyship because of the great difference in appearance, education and character of the two men. Roger was always slim and was born in Paris where he was brought up as a Frenchman until his middle teens; he later received a classical education at Stonehurst school in England. The impostor was coarse and fat, of little education (his spelling was atrocious), and possessed not the slightest knowledge of French. Nevertheless, when Lady Tichborne sent him not only a tidy sum of money, but also his fare to England, he decided to gamble on the outcome.

Before his departure Australian newspapers had publicised the story of Sir Roger Tichborne, Bart, being discovered at Wagga Wagga, and there was much excitement in Sydney's social circles with hostesses vying with each other to entertain him. In the meantime the scoundrel was endeavouring to gather what knowledge he could about the Tichborne family. In this respect he was fortunate, while in Sydney, to meet an old West Indian servant who had worked on the Tichborne estate and who provided him with useful information.

Orton, through his solicitor, had arranged to meet Lady Tichborne in Paris, but on his arrival in England he went first to Wapping to find his own family and offer his brothers and sisters life pensions to keep his secret. This settled, he travelled to Paris and made his way to the hotel where he had been booked in. There in his room he awaited with much apprehension the arrival of his 'mother'. Luck was with him all the way. An enraptured Dowager Lady Tichborne burst into the room and, throwing her arms around the fat neck of the impostor, exclaimed, 'My son! My dear lost son!'

It mattered not that the cultured voice of Sir Roger had changed to vulgar Cockney, that the well-bred gentleman's manners were now uncouth, the slim figure gross and ungainly, and that he could neither speak nor understand one word of the French language in which he had been so proficient. His handwriting bore no resemblance to that of the real Roger and, although when he was received by his close 'relatives' he made a brave attempt to identify them (having seen their portraits and photographs beforehand), he failed to recognise cousin Kate Doughty, who had been Roger's sweetheart since schooldays. But Lady Tichborne was not daunted. 'My poor dear Roger confuses everything in his head just as in a dream, and though his statements differ I believe him to be my son.' She promptly settled a suitable income on him until he should come into his large estates.

'Sir Roger' now played the country squire under the beaming gaze of his adoring 'mother'. The rest of the family refused to accept the scoundrel and would not admit him to their social circles. Matters came to a head when they decided on an examination of the claimant in Chancery. Strangely enough, the public was all for Orton and reiterated, 'Would not any mother recognise her own son?' Forty thousand pounds was raised by public subscription to finance his case, and two members of the House of Commons fought for his recognition as the rightful heir.

The Dowager Lady Tichborne was dead before the case eventually came to trial in May 1871, and it dragged on for almost a year. Long before the hearing was completed, the jury signified that it had gone far enough, and the Orton party was non-suited. Orton himself was committed for trial on a charge of perjury.

It seemed like the end, but it was not. The two members of the House of Commons were among a group which put up £10,000 to have Orton out on bail. 'In response to public pressure,' says a published report of the Tichborne case, 'the British Treasury defrayed the considerable expenses of Orton's witnesses who had to be called from South America and Australia.' At the trial before the Queen's

Bench of the Criminal Court, Orton was dismayed to find his ex-sweetheart from Wapping among the prosecution's witnesses. She not only identified him, but produced letters identifying his handwriting and poor spelling. She was followed by his brother Charles, to whom he had forgotten to pay the monthly allowance as the price for his silence. However, it was more than a year, in February 1874, before the impostor baronet was convicted and sentenced to fourteen years' penal servitude, despite the protests of his sympathetic public.

Orton was released ten years later, Parliament meanwhile having passed an Act declaring Sir Roger Doughty-Tichborne to be dead. After his release the former butcher from Wagga Wagga published a full confession of his guilt in the *People*, a London newspaper. He died three years later and was buried in a nameless grave on 1st April 1898— April Fool's Day.

Louis de Rougemont

Never has a more wonderful story of Australian adventures been written than *The Adventures of Louis de Rougemont,* 'as Told by Himself'. Little wonder that the story intrigued the world when it was published more than half a century ago; indeed it is so well told that it ranks among the most entrancing tales of its kind since the publication of *Robinson Crusoe.* Though not comparable in literary style with Defoe's masterpiece, and containing many absurdities and howlers, Louis de Rougemont's story is a rattling good adventure one.

The author claimed to have lived for thirty years among the Aborigines of unexplored northern Australia and to have married, according to tribal law, a full-blooded Aboriginal woman. In fact he dedicated his book 'To my devoted wife, Yamba, the noblest work of the Creator'. Until bitter criticism arose of the alleged truth of the adventures, de Rougemont was taken so seriously that he even gave lectures and read papers before members of the Geographical Society and the British Association for the Advancement of Science.

Oddly enough, the public was gullible about the tales of ghastly cannibal feasts, flying wombats, snake-charming, and of the author sleeping inside a dead buffalo to cure himself of fever and being unable to emerge when the hide shrunk. Nor were the accounts disbelieved of the faithful Yamba never leaving his side on his wanderings in Central Australia and elsewhere, bearing him numerous children and obligingly consenting to him taking the half-caste daughter of the lost explorer Leichhardt as a second wife. He dramatically told of Yamba killing and eating her baby in order to produce nourishment with which to suckle her sick husband during a fit of malaria.

All such things were believed. It was the items that happened to be true that made people scoff. For example de Rougemont told of riding on the backs of turtles—today a commonplace sport with tourists on some of the Great Barrier Reef islands—they refused point-blank to accept it.

The author first made his mark when, on arriving in London from Australia, he called on the editor of *Wide World Magazine* in Fleet Street, handed him a card with the name Count Louis de Rougemont on it and, taking a pinch of snuff, quietly announced in a cultured voice the object of mission. He began by regretting that he was unknown in England, his friends being in other lands. Friends he mentioned included Sir John Heaton and His Excellency Sir William Robinson, a former Governor of Western Australia, Count Louis de Rougemont said that he had just returned to civilisation after spending thirty years among the cannibals of unexplored Australia. He was wondering if the editor would be interested in his story.

The editor was so interested that three weeks later there appeared in the magazine the first instalment of 'The Adventures of Louis de Rougement, as Told by Himself'. Month after month the thrilling narrative unfolded, and the circulation of the magazine soared to record heights as adventure lovers of five continents eagerly awaited the next issue. Eventually the serial was published in book form.

One day in Sydney a Mrs Grin happened to see de Rougemont's book in a shop. The author's name meant nothing to her, but when she flicked its cover over and saw his photograph on the frontispiece she gasped in astonishment. It was a portrait of her wandering husband, Henri Grin. Armed with a copy of the book and enraged with its contents, it did not take Mrs Grin long to expose the villain. Soon newspaper journalists were at her home to interview her, and cables were sending their messages of the colossal fraud to every country. Mrs Grin remorselessly exposed this teller of tales.

The thirty-five-year-old wife said that she was born in Queensland, and that Henri was nearly twenty-five years her senior. They had four children—two boys, Charlie and Cecil, and two girls, Blanche and Gladys. When a journalist remarked that the latter names were those of the two shipwrecked girls her husband claimed in his book to have found in north-western Australia, Mrs Grin's indignation was understandable. Neither of her girls had ever been outside Sydney, much less survived a shipwreck.

The author's wife revealed that he, far from being a member of the French nobility, was born in Switzerland of peasant stock. She showed the journalists photographs of him as a boy taken with his parents outside their little farm cottage. Henri worked on the farm until he was sixteen, when he decided to see the world. Outlining his career, she said that he worked in many jobs and learnt enough English to get the position of footman with the famous English actress Fanny Kemble, with whom he stayed for seven years on her tours around the world. Butler, deck-hand, photographer, commercial traveller, he was even the inventor of a new kind of diving-suit which proved a failure.

Asked her opinion as to her husband's inspiration for his tall tales, Mrs Grin said that he was always reading books on travel and adventure. And, she reflected, he often told her about his first job when he came to this country. He was butler to the Governor of Western Australia, Sir William Robinson. One of the visitors to Government House was the explorer John Forrest, who at that time had just won the distinction of being the first to cross Australia from Perth to Adelaide.

While Henri was waiting at table, and pouring out the wines, he would hear the explorer telling of his adventures. His imagination kindled, Henri decided to see a little of the country outside the cities, so he left Government House and became a deck-hand on a cutter that went to Darwin. Afterwards he did another single trip in the same ship to North Queensland. But Mrs Grin was very definite that Henri never saw any of the inland country.

Regarding their married life, Mrs Grin said that her husband was always a dreamer, thinking up schemes that came to naught, and that she had to do the struggling with the cares and responsibilities of raising a family. She rarely received money from Henri, so it made little difference to her when he announced that he was going to New Zealand to search for copper. She thought he must have been successful in his search when recently, to her pleasant surprise, she received from him a remittance from London to the value of £30. Apparently it was a little of the royalties his writings were earning.

Despite the bubble-bursting of his reputation, Henri Grin, alias Count Louis de Rougemont, stuck to his story. He even appeared at the London Hippodrome riding a turtle in a tank: or rather, trying to demonstrate his capacity to do so. It was hardly a success, what with the fearful splashing and the difficulty of observing whether the man was on top of the turtle or vice versa. Undismayed, Henri returned to Australia to appear on the stage under the management of Harry Rickards, but his first appearance was his last. A pitiless hail of rude interjections smote and stung him, while stamping feet made his voice inaudible. Unable to make any headway against the storm of hostility, he made for safety in the shelter of the wings, his exit a permanent one.

This strange man, who could produce fiction founded upon fact that would rank with the world's best adventure yarns, ended his days in the infirmary of the Kensington workhouse in London and was buried in a pauper's grave.